CAMRA'S
YORKSHIRE
PUB WALKS

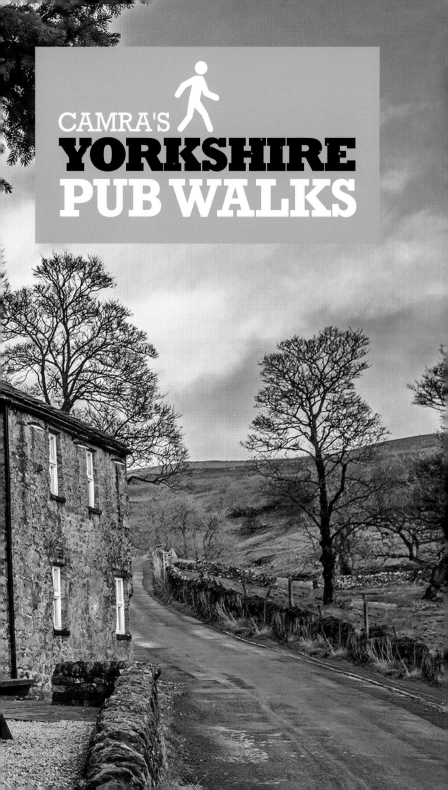

CAMRA'S YORKSHIRE PUB WALKS

CAMRA
BOOKS

Published by the Campaign for Real Ale Ltd.
230 Hatfield Road
St Albans
Hertfordshire AL1 4LW
www.camra.org.uk/books

Design and layout © Campaign for Real Ale Ltd. 2016
Text © Bob Steel

The right of Bob Steel to be identified as the author of this Work
has been asserted by him in accordance with the Copyright,
Designs and Patents Act 1988

ISBN 978-1-85249-329-5

Ordnance Survey Mapping is reproduced by permission
of HMSO. © Crown copyright 2016. All rights reserved. Ordnance
survey number 100047631

A CIP catalogue record for this book is available
from the British Library

Printed and bound in Slovenia by Latitude Press Ltd

Head of Publishing:	**Simon Hall**
Project Editor:	**Katie Button**
Editorial Assistance:	**Susannah Lord**
Design/Cartography:	**Stephen Bere**
Cover design:	**Stephen Bere**
Walk Locator Map:	**John Plumer**
	(JP Map Graphics Ltd)
Ordnance Survey	**The National Map Centre,**
mapping provided by:	**St Albans**
Sales & Marketing:	**David Birkett**

Photography: Bob Steel
Additional photography: Megan Allen/flickr p161 (top left),
p162 (bottom); Humphrey Bolton p17 (inset); Adam Bruderer/
flickr p75 (top), p94 (right); Bryan Ledgard/flickr p65 (bottom);
Chris Combe/flickr p69; James Cridland/flickr p93 (left); discov-
eryorkshirecoast.com/flickr p68; Tim Green/flickr p9, p89, p93
(right), p94 (left), p99, p101, p102, p103 (right), p104, p105, p122
(bottom), p125, p126 (left), p127, p128, p129, p130, p138-139;
Colin Gregory/flickr p43, 44; Cath Harries p140 (inset), p144
(top), p145, p146; johnthescone/flickr p133 (bottom), p136; Jules
& Jenny/flickr p163 (inset); Alex Liivet/flickr p10 (top); Smabs
Sputzer/flickr p73 (bottom); summonedbyfells/flickr p45 (top),
47 (bottom), 48 (right), p159; Michael Taylor p126 (right); Gary
Ullah/flickr p163; virtusincertus/flickr p58; Roger Ward/flickr p23
(inset); David Wright/flickr p161 (bottom)
Cover photography: steven gillis hd9 imaging/Alamy Stock
Photo (front cover, main); Hemis/Alamy Stock Photo (front cover,
inset); Tim Green/flickr (back cover, top); robertharding/Alamy
Stock Photo (back cover, bottom)

Acknowledgements
The author would like to thank all those who have helped in
the preparation of this guide, particularly to those members
of Yorkshire branches of the Campaign for Real Ale who have
contributed suggestions. These include Anne Berry, Rick Lamb,
Dave Pickersgill, Karl Smith, and David Street.

contents

North Yorkshire 11

West Yorkshire 75

City walks 137

Walk locator map

The walks in this guide have been grouped geographically: walks 1–10, coloured blue cover North Yorkshire, walks 11–20, coloured pink, are located in West and South Yorkshire, and walks 21–25, colored purple are urban walks. Many of the cities featured make a good base for walking day trips.

Contact details and opening hours for all the pubs are provided in the pub information boxes at the end of each route. Opening hours are correct at the time of writing. Where a pub offers accommodation, this has been indicated in the pub information box. Accommodation options range from camping barns to luxury bed and breakfast rooms. No assessment is made of quality or price.

KEY TO SYMBOLS USED IN THIS BOOK

Walk start
Walk route
Alternative route
Pub location
Compass point
Accommodation available

Introduction

Welcome to the sixth title in CAMRA's Pub Walks series, the first devoted to a single county. Yorkshire is England's largest county and Yorkshire folk are justifiably proud of it. It is the only one in Britain to contain two National Parks, and has several other areas of outstanding natural beauty as well as many fine cities.

Choosing a series of routes from such a wide area is always a challenge. As with other titles in the series the aim is to offer several pubs on each walk wherever possible, so that walkers can if they wish pick and choose how many, and what type of, pubs to visit.

I have tried to ensure that walks are accessible via public transport. In rural areas this can sometimes be difficult, and rural bus subsidies are being withdrawn in many areas. Using these services can only help to increase their viability so I would encourage it where possible. It also means you can all drink!

I have included some city walks, but elsewhere the selection of routes probably reflects my preferences for landscape. So I apologise to residents and devotees of the flatter landscapes of the south and east where there are distinctly fewer walks compared to the more dramatic landscapes of the South Pennines, Yorkshire Dales and Moors.

The walks have not been rigidly graded for difficulty as in many guides. Notes are included on the distance of the walk and any navigational difficulties, but in general the walks can often be shortened, perhaps by ordering a cab if buses are not to hand.

All the pubs listed in this guide should sell real ale in good condition. Many will be in your *Good Beer Guide*, but not all. This does not mean that the beer in the others will not be good: thanks in part to CAMRA's relentless campaigning, quality is probably better now than it has ever been, and many parts of Yorkshire have more pubs selling good beer than can fit in the Guide! Remember though that pubs do change – landlords come and go, so do staff. Please remember too that the range of beer in a particular pub may change – so take the notes about beers on offer at any pub as indicative rather than definitive! In general you will have plenty of choice.

As an unapologetic enthusiast of traditional unspoilt pubs I have also tried to include as many of CAMRA's 'Real Heritage pubs' as is possible in these pages. For those who share

The rolling Wensleydale landscape

my interest in such premises I would warmly recommend *Yorkshire's Real Heritage Pubs*, also published by CAMRA. It's an authoritative, but very readable companion to the social history, geography and architecture of the Yorkshire pub with a scholarly eye for the features which make them distinctive. I have found it a great companion whilst compiling this guide.

Opening times

Midday is the normal opening time for most pubs but lunchtime closures are common notably in rural areas, and some pubs have restricted winter hours. Opening times for the pubs are correct at the time of writing but I would advise phoning ahead if there is any doubt, or if it's critical that a particular pub is open; nothing is worse than a pub walk visiting closed pubs! Timing tips are given for the routes to assist you in making the most of them; I always recommend doing a bit of planning ahead, especially if you have some distance to cover before starting the walk. All routes are accessible by public transport, and this information is given for each walk.

Food of course is now widely available in pubs; and the majority of pubs in this book offer at least snacks and sandwiches. I refer to food on offer on these walks, although I have not religiously included food information for each pub. If you want to eat whilst on one of these trails, you should have no trouble, unless you decide to go at a very busy time or late in the evening. If in doubt, phone ahead.

Before you set out

For countryside walks a reasonable level of fitness is required. None of the walks venture into really wild country, but although there are ways to shorten many of the walks either on foot or on public transport, there are steep hills in places and you will encounter rough ground, so it is your responsibility to ensure you are fit enough and properly equipped. Never venture out without rainwear since the sunniest day can quickly turn. I strongly recommend walking boots with ankle support and would advise you not to wear trainers or street shoes. You may find a pair of walking poles useful for stability on rough ground or crossing stepping stones.

Always carry water, and some spare food, such as chocolate or other snacks. I like to take a flask with me if I'm unlikely to pass a café before arriving at the first pub.

Navigation can sometimes present problems even with a good map, and although we include Ordnance Survey map extracts showing the routes I would recommend carrying the appropriate sheet of the map (or digital equivalent) as a back up and for wider orientation. The necessary sheets of the 1:25,000 'Explorer' series are given in the information box at the start of all the non-urban walks. All the routes have been personally surveyed every step of the way so I would hope that difficulties are reduced to a minimum. If things do go wrong it's normally fairly easy to make for the nearest road or other landscape feature.

Midnight Bell, Leeds

Yorkshire: The geography and geology of the county for walkers

England's largest county encompasses not only a wide variety of natural landscapes – after all, three of our dozen national parks lie wholly or partially within the county – but also a human legacy that contributes to the county's charm for walkers.

The Pennine chain forms the backdrop to Yorkshire's geography: it divides it physically from its old rival Lancashire, and it gives rise to a network of rivers which have carved much of the county's physical landscape. Moreover these rivers powered the early industrial development of the region and in turn left a rich historical legacy.

Industrial Yorkshire

Within Yorkshire the southern part of the Pennines is composed, on the surface, of a tough sandstone known as Millstone Grit. Fast-flowing streams running off to the east were exploited by mills, and the soft water running off the sandstone was ideal for washing fleeces. This led to the development of an important woollen textile industry. Towns like

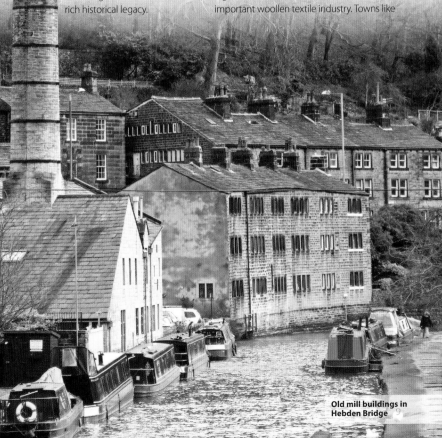

Old mill buildings in Hebden Bridge

Heptonstall and Hebden Bridge (**Walk 11**) are great examples of settlements associated with the woollen industry.

Later, the discovery of coal seams at the foothills east of the Pennines gave rise to industry on a far larger scale. Bradford became the centre, supported by a chain of industrial towns like Halifax and Huddersfield, Bingley and Keighley. These towns, surrounded by picturesque hilly landscape are traditionally built of sandstone, giving a distinctive appearance to the area and making for excellent walking country. This is exemplified in **walks 13 to 18**. A similar pattern of development occurred in Sheffield where metal-working rather than woollens became the chief industry. The Kelham Island Industrial Museum (**Walk 23**) traces the industrial history of Sheffield.

A distinctive white phone box in Hull

Rural Yorkshire

The northern half of the Yorkshire Pennines, north of Skipton, presents a remarkably different appearance. Here, the surface geology is the distinctive Carboniferous limestone, with outcrops of the light grey rock overlain with few trees except in valleys, and much open landscape with wide glaciated valleys. **Walks 1 to 6** are set in this limestone country. Being away from the coalfields and giving rise to hard water this area was never heavily industrialised; today much of this part of the county is protected as the Yorkshire Dales National Park. This is also the reason why Leeds, the largest city in West Yorkshire, never became a woollen textile manufacturer.

Yorkshire Dales landscape

Its river, the Aire, was a hard water stream. Instead, Leeds diversified into other industries and became the administrative centre for the textile industry as well as a major brewing town which, of course, will always be associated with Tetley's brewery, which closed in 2011. Today the city centre is undergoing a renaissance reflected in the exciting new canalside bars (**Walk 22**).

Moving away from the Pennines, Yorkshire is dissected north to south by a wide vale of lowland and relatively unspectacular landscape. It is nonetheless home to several of Yorkshire's finest market towns, notably Northallerton, Thirsk, Ripon, Selby and Malton. The market town of Beverley (**Walk 24**) with its stunning Minster offers a flavour of the ambience of this group of towns. And at the focus of this vale, a natural centre as well as ecclesiastical and administrative hub, lies York itself with its medieval city walls (**Walk 21**).

The sandstone uplands of the North York Moors (the county's other National Park) offers a landscape quite different to the western gritstone: exposed moorland in its centre, surrounded by undulating and still very rural countryside especially on its northern side (**Walks 8 and 9**). Look out for the distinctive orange pantiles on the roofs of older buildings here and towards the coast, a relic of the Flemish influence on eastern England.

The Yorkshire coast

The coastal ports of Yorkshire are represented in this volume by two contrasting places. Whitby, (**Walk 10**) is an atmospheric old town famous as a whaling centre but still a working port today with perhaps the largest concentration of fish and chip shops known to man. Hull (**Walk 25**) is a one-off in so many ways with its own telephone boxes, its own trains and an independence which must come from its relative isolation. Having seen its fishing industry devastated in the last fifty years Hull has reinvented itself fairly successfully and an exploration of its old town makes a very rewarding urban walk.

North Yorkshire

Settle & Upper Ribblesdale

Ribblesdale is a personal favourite among the valleys of the Yorkshire Dales, and this circuit out from Settle offers a satisfying taste of the variety of scenery that characterises limestone country: a wide green valley, rocky outcrops, bleak but atmospheric moorland, and solidly attractive hamlets. All this knitted together by the well-worn framework of dry-stone walls and presided over by one of the Dales' much-loved 'Three Peaks', Pen-y-Ghent. Two well-spaced pubs on the round and a couple of decent drinking options in Settle itself, make this a satisfying and easily accessible walk. Navigation is generally fairly straightforward, but the morning walk over from Stackhouse to Feizor needs a little care and a compass might offer reassurance.

▶ **Start:** Settle river bridge

▶ **Finish:** Settle town centre

▶ **Access:** Settle–Carlisle railway from Leeds/Bradford

▶ **Distance:** 12.8 miles (20.8 km) for full circuit, 8.7 miles with short cut

▶ **OS map:** Explorer OL2

▶ **Key attractions:** Settle–Carlisle railway (www.settle-carlisle.co.uk)

▶ **THE PUBS:** Game Cock, Austwick; Helwith Bridge Inn, Helwith Bridge; Lion at Settle, Talbot Arms, both Settle

▶ **Timing tips:** A visit to Elaine's tea rooms at Feizor is highly recommended, so allow up to three hours to cover the five miles or so from Settle to Austwick, where the Game Cock opens all day from 11.30am except Mondays, when it's closed all day. If you're taking the short-cut route omitting the Game Cock, the tea rooms also sell bottled beers!

Field barn near Feizor

KEY

🚶 Walk start/finish

– – – Walk route

•••••• Alternative route

Alternative short route

🚶 Start the walk from the river bridge, which officially divides Settle and its twin town of Giggleswick. It's easy to get there from the station and it's about five minutes' walk from Settle's compact market place. Cross to the Giggleswick side and bear onto the Ribble Way path almost immediately, leading between a football ground and the school to join the riverside.

Settle is quickly left behind and it's a pleasant and easy half-mile along the river floodplain to join the quiet lane near Stackhouse. En route you'll see the chimneys of the old mills at Langcliffe, adding picturesque variety to the landscape (see box). Cross the road to go through the gate opposite and walk along the wall towards the trees ahead,

where the road bends to the right. The path heads uphill along the wall, but once through most of the trees a Land Rover track joins the path, where the wall peels off to the right. Head uphill here between two single trees on an indistinct path, but look for a step stile left of a lone tree at the top of the first rise, then make for a pair of metal gates.

Take the left-hand gate and follow the grassy track which winds uphill to the left, as far as a gate in a wall (**A** 🕐 807662). Follow the wall, still in a north-westerly direction, to a gate at the far end and then through a wooden gate just beyond, which opens out onto a good grass track continuing northwest. This is the most remote stretch of the walk, but in poor weather it's reassuring to know that the café at Feizor is only about a

Game Cock, Austwick

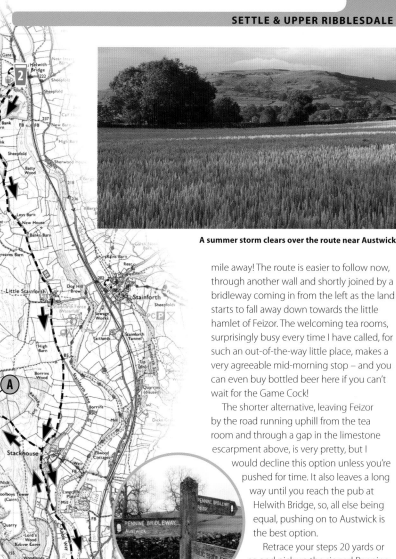

A summer storm clears over the route near Austwick

mile away! The route is easier to follow now, through another wall and shortly joined by a bridleway coming in from the left as the land starts to fall away down towards the little hamlet of Feizor. The welcoming tea rooms, surprisingly busy every time I have called, for such an out-of-the-way little place, makes a very agreeable mid-morning stop – and you can even buy bottled beer here if you can't wait for the Game Cock!

The shorter alternative, leaving Feizor by the road running uphill from the tea room and through a gap in the limestone escarpment above, is very pretty, but I would decline this option unless you're pushed for time. It also leaves a long way until you reach the pub at Helwith Bridge, so, all else being equal, pushing on to Austwick is the best option.

Retrace your steps 20 yards or so and pick up the signed Pennine Bridleway, which heads off to the right on a charming little walled grass lane (Hale Lane on the map) that leads through chocolate-box landscape, passing some ruins and crossing a stream after about half a mile. Shortly after this, with the village clearly visible to your left, look for a step stile in the wall on the left; keep parallel with the wall across the field to join another walled lane, in turn joining a motor road leading into Austwick. On the left you pass the Traddock, an upmarket hotel that is open

15

The hamlet of Stackhouse in early morning light

to the public and offers at least one real ale (usually from Three Peaks brewery); but you may feel underdressed in your boots and rucksack. In any case, it's now just 200 yards (right at the junction with the main street) to the 🍺 **Game Cock**, the pleasant village pub. This traditional Thwaites house has a largish restaurant area at the front, but there is a pleasant old-fashioned drinkers' bar with an open fire and a recent extension has added two further small rooms without spoiling the

atmosphere. The four handpulls dispense Thwaites beers as this is a tied house, but one sometimes offers a guest. You'll probably be interested in food by now, and happily the place offers an all-day menu.

Walk north along the road as far as the northern extremity of the village where, clearly signed, the Pennine Bridleway ('Feizor') leads off to the right by a converted field barn. Head down here to a small stream crossed by a tiny clapper bridge. After persistent rain this crossing can still give you wet feet and *in extremis* you may need to return to the road and walk round (consult the map); a few yards beyond, a clear path leaves via a step stile on the left and cuts across fields (make for the solitary tree) to rejoin Wood Lane, the walled bridleway you left to enter Austwick (**B** 🕐 777685). On reaching this, almost immediately opposite the path continues uphill, through a couple of gates. Keep the dry-stone wall closely on your left to follow the right of way as far as Jop Ridding house, where the right of way becomes a vehicle track and leads you easily to rejoin the road. Turn to your right and then, just

before you reach Newfield House and barn, leave the road on the path ('Horton-in-Ribblesdale') to the left, up to a step stile in the first wall and a ladder stile in the next, then keep right along the edge of a small ridge with the old Dry Rigg quarry down to your left. Descend to the quarry road and left for 30 yards to rejoin the motor road again, and now it's just a few minutes downhill to the tiny hamlet of Helwith Bridge and the eponymous inn adjacent to the railway.

The **2 Helwith Bridge Inn** is a welcoming, unpretentious pub, which, being in the heart of Three Peaks country, has a long pedigree catering for outdoor types. It offers just what the weary walker needs: a great range of well-kept beers and hearty food at reasonable

THE LANGCLIFFE MILLS

There have been mills on the Langcliffe stretch of the River Ribble since the Middle Ages, the originals having been built by the monks of Furness Abbey. Watershed Mill, the closest to Settle, dates back to 1785 and, like the larger High Mill further north, was built as a cotton mill. After a brief period as a weaving mill and closure during the 1850s, both mills were reconverted to spinning in 1861 and had a successful spell drawing in workers as young as 10 years old from as far as Cornwall. By the 1930s, High Mill employed 250 people, with another 100 at Watershed Mill. Both mills closed in the early 1950s. Watershed Mill was initially purchased by corn merchants, who used it as a warehouse, but it was eventually bought by the Edinburgh Woollen Mill and turned into a shopping centre of sorts; while High Mill is now occupied by a packaging company.

prices. Thwaites Original is a fixture, but there are always guest beers, notably from Settle's Three Peaks brewery, which also supplies the house beer.

Feizor nestles under a steep limestone scar

Now from the Helwith Bridge there are several options. You could call for a cab or, if you like it here, you could stay adjacent in the campsite or the *Hotel Paradiso* – ask the landlord! If you have your own map and the train timetable, a pleasant option is to walk up to Horton-in-Ribblesdale station for the train back to Settle (see box).

The route mapped out, back to Settle on foot, is almost a four-mile walk, much of it on road, albeit the pleasant and lightly trafficked lane crossed on the way out. Simply head back up the hill, following the telegraph lines up a track to the left in a few minutes to make a good short cut, then south, passing Little Stainforth halfway. You can cut off the loop of Stainforth Lane south of Little Stainforth by taking a gently rising path on the right round to the west of the hamlet of Stackhouse, rejoining your outward route over the fields to emerge at the road bridge.

Back in Settle, walk up into town and the Market Place. The two best drinking options in this pretty little town are both very close by. The **3 Lion at Settle** is a short way down Duke Street (the main road) on the left. This 17th-century former coaching inn has two high-ceilinged rooms, a wood-panelled main bar with its huge fireplace and impressive staircase, and a smaller side room off the bar. Choose from a range of Thwaites beers

🚶 WALKING ROUTE TO HORTON STATION

The walk north to Horton-in-Ribblesdale for the train to Settle is about two miles, so allow plenty of time. It's not shown on our map so ensure you have the OS map with you. Head out of the car park and turn immediately right down the quarry road (or cut across the camping field by the stile next to the *Hotel Paradiso*). Walk down the road (or adjacent margin) to the rail bridge, then follow the right of way under here to the river and up to Cragg Hill Farm. Take care: (i) do not cross the river on the footbridge, and (ii) shortly after, the fenced lane becomes impassable and the right of way runs along the fields immediately to the left – look for the way marks, stile and gates. At Cragg Hill Farm it's easy, all the way into Horton on the farm road, emerging conveniently by the path up to the station.

or opt for one of the guests, usually locally sourced. You can eat here (there's a separate dining room) or in the equally appealing **4 Talbot Arms**, an attractive whitewashed building round to the right from the Lion in the High Street, just off the square. A family-run free house offering several guest beers (and real cider) sourced from the north of the region, the Talbot has a pleasant terraced beer garden to the rear which, if the weather permits, makes a good spot to relax and study the map over a pint before catching the train home. Food is available until 8pm.

PUB INFORMATION

1 GAME COCK
Austwick, LA2 8B •
01524 251226 • www.gamecockinn.co.uk
Opening hours: closed Mon; 11.30 (12 Sat & Sun)-11

2 HELWITH BRIDGE INN
Helwith Bridge, BD24 0EH •
01729 860220 • www.helwithbridgeinn.co.uk
Opening hours: 12-midnight

3 LION AT SETTLE
Duke Street, Settle, BD24 9DU •
01729 822203
www.thelionsettle.co.uk
Opening hours: 11-11.30 (midnight Fri & Sat); 12-11.30 Sun

4 TALBOT ARMS
High Street, Settle, BD24 9EX
01729 823924 • www.talbotsettle.co.uk
Opening hours: 12-11

The Ribble at Stainforth

Ribblehead & Three Peaks country

WALK 2

Even in a county as large and varied as Yorkshire, few if any areas can surpass the grandeur of the wilder parts of the Dales, and this walk between two of the county's biggest hills is deservedly popular. The frequently changing light and weather conditions here make the scenery continually interesting and, by establishing a couple of welcoming pubs centrally within this landscape, man has added to what nature has provided. The iconic Settle–Carlisle railway both augments the man-made landscape and provides a convenient means of access to this still-remote area. To enjoy all aspects of this route at its best, ensure you arrive at the Old Hill Inn when it's open! Allow a good two hours, possibly more, to reach the pub from Ribblehead, less if you try the route in reverse. If you want more of a challenge, there is an option to detour via Whernside.

▶ **Start/finish:** Ribblehead station (or nearby car park)

▶ **Access:** Settle–Carlisle railway from Leeds/Bradford. Summer Sunday/bank holiday bus 831 only (see www.dalesbus.org)

▶ **Distance:** 7.4 miles (12 km)

▶ **OS map:** Explorer OL2

▶ **Key attractions:** Settle–Carlisle railway (www.settle-carlisle.co.uk); England's most famous railway viaduct; classic limestone landscape between two highest peaks in the Dales National Park

▶ **THE PUBS:** Old Hill Inn, Chapel-le-Dale; Station Inn, Ribblehead

▶ **Timing tips:** The Old Hill Inn is closed on Mondays, and between 3pm and 6pm on other weekdays. If coming from Leeds, trains are every two hours; the 8.49 may be a tough call but will deposit you at Ribblehead shortly after 10am, an ideal starting time.

Winterscales farm has views over the valley

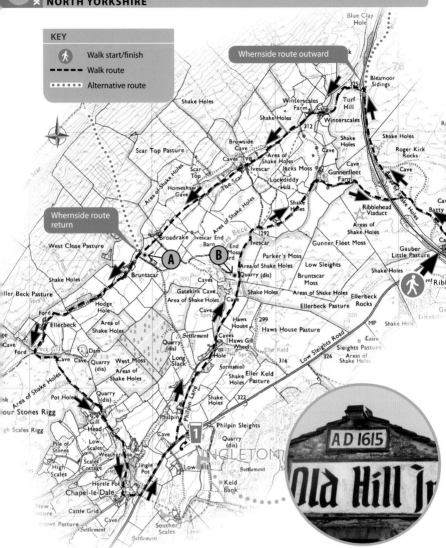

KEY

🚶 Walk start/finish
- - - - Walk route
• • • • • • Alternative route

Whernside route outward

Whernside route return

AD 1615

Ola Hill Jr

🚶 The natural way to start the walk is to arrive by the scenic Settle–Carlisle railway. The northbound platform is new, the original having been removed during the dark days of the 80s when the line was a hair's breadth from final closure. Walk down to the road and, passing the Station Inn (which we will save for later!), bear left on the bridleway striking off towards the famous Ribblehead viaduct. If arriving by car, park in the car park by the junction of the two roads

just east of the station and join the route via the footpath signed 'Bleamoor sidings' across the road.

Approaching the viaduct you reach a plaque marking the site where here, on Blea Moor common (or Batty Moss), a shanty town housing workers on the line and the viaduct once stood. At the point where the path forks, keep right (signed 'Whernside'). You'll be passing under the viaduct later in the walk, so you can inspect it at closer hand

The Old Hill Inn is a welcome sight

then, should you wish. Ascend to follow the railway line until, just before reaching the lonely Blea Moor signal box, you reach a path junction, where our main route turns sharp left under the railway. If you are taking in Whernside – the highest of Yorkshire's Three Peaks – using your own map or guide-book, keep straight on here and return to the route later on near Bruntscar at point A.

The path now makes for and follows a line of farms sited along a relatively rich ribbon of land at the foot of the Whernside massif ahead. The first is Winterscales with great views now opening out of the wide valley and of Ingelborough Hill, the distinctive flat-topped mountain dominating the view. At Ivescar continue ahead on the bridleway (signed 'Scar End'), which now leaves the tarmac and becomes a grass track through a gate immediately left of the more obvious track with its 'private' sign. Cross fields with a wonderful view back to the viaduct and Pen-y-Ghent (the last of the Three Peaks) beyond. Look out for gates and keep to the *bon chemin* as you head towards the next farmstead, Broadrake.

**Whernside under a dusting
of winter snow**

Just beyond (**A** 739790), the Three Peaks Walk route joins from the right and then heads off left to the Old Hill Inn but, perversely, we keep straight ahead once more and continue through the tiny hamlet of Bruntscar with its partially ruined old Hall. Shortly there is a gentle

The enigmatic inscription below the statue in Chapel-le-Dale

climb up to the final farm on this section, Ellerbeck. Just beyond here by a gate and a signpost ('Scar End 3¼') cross a ford and take the rough lane as it swings to the left and makes its way down to the valley bottom. Views down the valley are quite superb, particularly if you've chosen a bright, clear day. As you enter the plantation and

just beyond Gillhead House look out for the 'Statue' with its interesting plaque (and the chilly warning about the spirit of the mysterious Boggard!); and, lower down, the lovely little St Leonards Church in Chapel-le-Dale. It's well worth a visit if it's open – note the memorial to workers killed on the construction of the railway.

From here walk the last 100 yards left down to the road junction, from which it's a short uphill walk on the relatively busy B6255 road to the first call of the day, the **Old Hill Inn**. Remember the rule of the road for walkers: walk on the right, facing the traffic, in single file.

St Leonards Church, Chapel-le-Dale

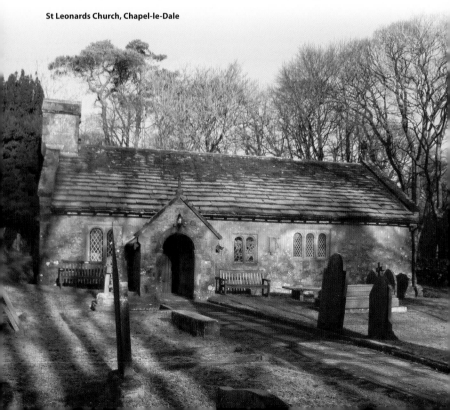

The well-known inn dates from 1615 and has offered hospitality to many generations of hikers and potholers. The interior, though carefully restored, reflects its location at a focus of paths heading up to the two nearby big hills (and down to extensive cave systems): no over-fussy décor, and fittings of a more rough-hewn style, with exposed stonework competing with the timber. Alongside the portfolio of local beers including a couple from nearby Dent, good-quality food is served and the menu is extensive.

On leaving the Hill Inn, retrace your steps about 100 yards down the road and turn very sharp right up the farm track (which, despite the absence of signage, is a right of way), passing the nondescript modern house and then Philpin Farm. As the farm road bends left beyond the farm by a cattle grid, the signed bridleway now leaves to the left up a stream bed, which is at best muddy and may be partially under water, in which case you may have to take to the field immediately before it to avoid the water. At the far end of this short and enclosed section you need to leave by the gate on the left and head through a field and further gates, at which point the route ahead is rather indistinct: aim across the narrow stream to the left of a group of four trees ahead and then you'll pick up a clear path once again, keeping alongside a wall on the right to join a narrow tarmac farm track at (**B** ⊙ **747788**). Keep on this road in the same northerly direction

RIBBLEHEAD VIADUCT

Possibly the country's most well-known structure of its kind, Ribblehead is the scenic highlight of the Settle–Carlisle railway but was also almost the cause of its downfall. 440 yards long, and 104 feet above the valley at its highest point, it has 24 arches and climbs gently towards its northern end. A large shanty town was constructed to house the navvies when it was built in what was a remote and inaccessible area in the early 1870s. In the 1980s when the line was under threat of closure, it was the cost of maintaining the viaduct that was most often cited as the main problem of keeping the line open. A vigorous campaign succeeded in winning the day and today the line is not only a very popular tourist route but also a vital lifeline for local people, a busy freight artery and an important strategic alternative to the West Coast mainline.

The Duchess of Sutherland on Ribblehead viaduct

Ingleborough Hill

bearing right ('Ribblehead') and right again by the large barns to pass right under the Ribblehead viaduct. The sheer size and durability of this structure fills one with awe when you remember that the Victorian workmen had little of the technology and mechanical assistance that we enjoy today; yet the viaduct was used as the primary excuse to try and close the line thirty years ago.

Retrace your outward route now to reach the welcome of the **2** **Station Inn** right by the railway embankment. This wonderfully situated pub has been given a much-needed dose of TLC in recent years after a rather neglected period. It now majors on an extensive menu, to which end the former main bar has been converted into a dining area, while the room to the left has been brought into use for casual drinkers. The latter are nonetheless well served with a decent range of ales, including the house beer brewed by Copper Dragon alongside changing guests.

From here the station is but five minutes' walk – reassuring in poor weather.

Welcome fire in the Station Inn

PUB INFORMATION

1 **OLD HILL INN** •
Chapel-le-Dale, LA6 3AR •
01524 241256 • www.oldhillinn.co.uk
Opening hours: closed Mon; 12-3, 6-11; 12-11 Sat

2 **STATION INN** •
Ribblehead, Ingleton, LA6 3AS •
01524 241274
www.thestationinn.net
Opening hours: 11-midnight; 12-11 Sun

Down the Wharfe from Grassington

Pretty Grassington is rightly regarded as the capital of Upper Wharfedale and, while the (currently under threat) local bus service still operates, it also provides a good base for several of the walks in this volume. This fairly easy circuit makes for the pleasant Dales village of Appletreewick with two closely adjacent real ale pubs, including the atmospheric Craven Arms with its classic multi-roomed interior. There are options to visit other good establishments on or close to the route, and, if you're based locally, I'd recommend the Fountaine Inn at Linton for its setting alone. As befits the lovely Wharfe valley the scenery is excellent throughout, and navigation of the route is pretty straightforward.

▸ **Start/finish:** Grassington village

▸ **Access:** Via Skipton or Ilkley via local bus services (www.prideofthedales.co.uk; www.dalesbus.org/874.html)

▸ **Distance:** 7.4 miles (12 km)

▸ **OS map:** Explorer OL2

▸ **Key attractions:** Bolton Abbey (www.boltonabbey.com; 5 miles); Parcevall Hall Gardens (www.parcevall-hallgardens.co.uk); unspoilt valley with fine scenery; Grassington and Burnsall villages; Linton Falls; Dales Way riverside path

▸ **THE PUBS:** Craven Arms, Appletreewick; Clarendon Hotel, Hebden; Foresters Arms, Grassington. Try also: New Inn, Appletreewick; Fountaine Inn, Linton

▸ **Timing tips:** The Craven Arms opens at 11am, so an early start from Grassington is feasible. The Clarendon at Hebden shuts from 3pm until 6pm on weekdays, so if you aim to visit, plan accordingly.

Kail Lane , a walled bridleway en route to Appletreewick

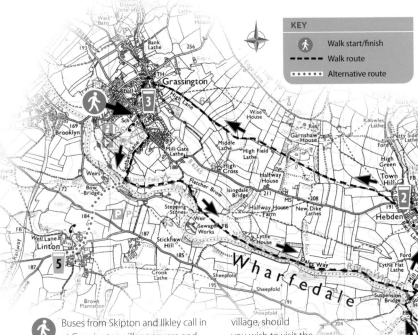

Buses from Skipton and Ilkley call in at Grassington village square and also at the National Park Centre, five minutes away on foot from where the walk starts. Here, you can find local information and toilets before you get on your way.

Take quiet Sedber Lane at the far end of the car park – it leads to a walled path down to the river and to Linton Falls. Like all waterfalls these are far more impressive after heavy rain, but whatever the weather it's a pleasant spot. It's also (by crossing the bridge) the quickest walking route to Linton village, should you wish to visit the Fountaine Inn later.

The walk in hand, however, stays on the north bank of the Wharfe; follow it downstream through meadows, soon passing a trout farm before reaching a gate and signpost where you follow the direction to Burnsall across another meadow to rejoin the river along a pretty, partially wooded section. The flat areas on each side of the river channel hereabouts are river terraces, usually associated with historic

The suspension bridge over the Wharfe near Hebden

changes in relative sea level. After a mile or so, you'll reach an interesting suspension footbridge (do not cross), where you head to the left to join a quiet lane in about 50 yards. Now bear right as far as a signed path ('Hebden') just over the river bridge, which leads you past some houses and gardens, all in an enviable, tucked-away location, before the path leads through a short, wooded section and emerges by another signpost with several options. Take that (signed 'Hartlington & Raikes') which cuts back acutely to the right to a stile in the wall, and cross this to the buildings of Ranelands Farm a couple of hundred yards away. Go through the farmyard and then head up the slope ahead (no obvious worn path, but a field barn is visible on the horizon), passing one or two ancient muckspreaders assembled on the sward at the foot of the slope. The gate is in the top right

New Inn, Appletreewick

corner of this field; keep well to the right of the field barn but pause to take in the wide rural views that have opened up behind you, more than ample reward for the effort on this stiff but short ascent.

Once a couple of solitary trees come into view, make towards these; and when you hit the wall, follow it to the stile in the far corner. Now it's simple, following the signs to take you onto the road by South View Farm, thence bearing right on the quiet lane down to Raikes Farm. From here it's a pleasant road walk down the hill (ignore the side turning for Hebden) to the 'main'

Caravan from yesteryear, Hartlington

Inside the Craven Arms

road at the foot of the hill. Note the ancient motor caravan in the garden by the junction!

Turn left for Appletreewick. Although it's hardly a busy road, take care on the narrow Hartlington Bridge, where sight lines are limited, then climb uphill a short way to the point where a signed bridleway leads off to the left. This is Kail Lane. Head up here for the longest ascent of the day (but on the whole at a pretty gentle angle), carrying you up onto the pasturelands above the valley of the Barden Beck. Pass some agricultural buildings, where the path veers a little to the left, and reach a signed path heading right for Appletreewick a few minutes further on. Disregard this first path: it's a more satisfying descent into the village to continue along the moor for another few minutes. The wide stony track veers to the left but at this point continue straight ahead to a substantial wall, keeping it on your immediate right. As a study of the map shows, the landscape here is strewn with old lead-mine workings, just as in many limestone areas of the Peak District.

Just before reaching the far corner of this large field (**A** 🌲 058609), an easily over-looked step stile in the wall (by a decrepit old post topped with faded yellow paint) leads you into a small paddock. Care is needed here as there are two paths leading from

it: disregard the obvious one marked by a ladder stile and, instead, cross to the bottom right corner of this paddock where another step stile in a wall takes you into a larger field and gently downhill along the wall, as far as yet another step stile taking you into a long, narrow field. Now the way is clear, with another stile on the lower side of this field visible which leads down and into a walled and wooded lane, a pleasant surprise after a morning in a very open landscape.

It's an excellent descent into Appletree-wick, which you'll reach in another few min-utes. On meeting the road at the eastern end of the village, bear right and walk down the village street, passing one or two interesting buildings. Look out particularly for Mock Beg-gar Hall, a lovely listed building on the right-hand (north) side. Also known as Monks Hall, the building is associated with nearby Bolton Priory, having once been a grange for that monastic house. Note the carved stone head above the door, but also the numerous holes above the windows which almost certainly were for pigeons, often kept for their meat and their eggs.

Not far beyond this is the **4 New Inn**, listed here as a 'try also' option since (i) it may not be open if you've set out early from Grassington (the nearby Craven Arms opens at 11am) and (ii) though a perfectly good hostelry, I would not promote it at the expense of the latter, should you wish to take in only one Appletreewick pub. The interior is modern, with a dining room and bar, but there's a real fire for winter and some well-sited outdoor tables at the front offering fine views. Up to five cask beers are available, with Goose Eye's Chinook a regular fixture, alongside a real cider and a very good range of foreign bottled beers. Food is available all day from opening at noon.

The **Craven Arms** is 300 yards further down the road. It's named for Appletreewick's most famous son, William Craven, born to paupers in 1548 but who went on to own the Merchant Tailors and become Lord Mayor of London before returning to his native village, restoring the High Hall and improving local communications. He was knighted and his descendants became the Earls of Craven. The pub itself is a fitting legacy in its own right: a wonderful old building with atmosphere aplenty, a multi-roomed free house with stone-flagged floors, oak beams and gas lighting. Both the main bar room and the lovely taproom have ancient fireplaces, furniture and fittings. At the rear and well worth a look is the exceptionally well-executed, traditionally constructed cruck barn (all of a decade old!), and on the way is a delightful

little snug. For the inner man and woman there's a wide-ranging menu showcasing local producers and, of course, an excellent selection of beers (with a strong Yorkshire focus) including local brewer Dark Horse's fine Hetton Pale and Craven Bitter. A top-notch place, not to be missed.

The return leg of the walk starts with a long and very attractive riverside stretch; but if you are walking on a weekday and planning to stop at the Clarendon at Hebden, refer to the opening times and (allowing up to two hours' walking to get there) plan your departure time accordingly.

Walk a little further down the lane as far as Masons campsite, where you pick up the signed path down to the riverside. It's a very relaxing and pleasant walk all the way into Burnsall, following the river most of way but clearly signed whenever necessary. Enter the village across a manicured meadow followed by walking over the handsome stone bridge, built by William Craven. Burnsall is a substantial village that looks just a little over-prettified, and much the same could be said about the village 'pub', the Red Lion, which is aimed squarely at the well-heeled residential trade; but you'll be able to get a beer if you need one before continuing on the riverside path, which is accessed by a sharp right turn after crossing the bridge.

The Wharfe near Appletreewick

Foresters Arms, Grassington

Now it's another very pleasant riverside walk passing some appealing limestone crags (with plenty of opportunities for an afternoon siesta if you need one) before you find yourself back at the suspension bridge once again. Cross (single file only!) and head back up the lane again. This time I recommend you simplify matters by bearing left along the quiet road that winds up into Hebden (but, if you prefer, you can follow the morning path up to the village instead with the aid of the map and the path signs).

Once at the main road junction you'll spot the impressive frontage of the **2 Clarendon Hotel** to your left. It's a family-run affair, in quite an imposing building for what is a small and quiet village. The lounge bar caters for diners and drinkers alike, and offers up to four guest beers from the likes of Black Sheep, Thwaites or Marston's. The front outside seating is popular in summer despite the passing traffic.

It's about a mile and a half back to Grassington. Walk up the road a short way and take the second of two signed paths on the right, to 'Grassington via High Lane'. The way ahead is pretty straightforward now, across fields for the first part with a lot of negotiation of stiles but some pretty flower meadows to enjoy in summer; and down into Grassington via the walled High Lane, which

disgorges you into the top end of the village. Grassington has several pubs – if you want to round off the walk with another glass or two I suggest you make for the **3 Foresters Arms** on Main Street (through a small alley from the more prominent Black Horse). It's a spacious free house with a range of Yorkshire staples (Timothy Taylor's Landlord, Tetley, Black Sheep, etc) on the bar but with rarer and/or more interesting beers like Tetley Mild and Wharfedale Blonde in support. There's an extensive food menu alongside and, once again, some sun-trap tables on the front courtyard if the weather permits.

From the Foresters it's a very short downhill stroll to the market place or, five minutes beyond, the National Park Centre. But finally, as I suggested earlier, should you be staying locally, a visit to the nearby **5 Fountaine Inn** at Linton is recommended. The setting, on a lovely village green, is idyllic, and the handsome stone building still retains some internal character. You'll have a good choice of beers, too, with Wharfedale Blonde and Dark Horse Hetton Pale, alongside more familiar names like Thwaites Bitter.

PUB INFORMATION

1 CRAVEN ARMS
Appletreewick, BD23 6DA
01756 720270 • www.craven-cruckbarn.co.uk
Opening hours: 11-11; 11-10.30 Sun

2 CLARENDON HOTEL
Hebden, BD23 5DE •
01756 752446 • www.clarendonhebden.co.uk
Opening hours: 12-3, 6-11; 11-11 Sat & Sun

3 FORESTERS ARMS
20 Main Street, Grassington, BD23 5AA •
01756 752349 • www.forestersarmsgrassington.co.uk
Opening hours: 12-midnight (1am Fri & Sat)

Try also:

4 NEW INN
Main Street, Appletreewick, BD23 6DA •
01756 720252 • www.the-new-inn-appletreewick.com
Opening hours: 12-11

5 FOUNTAINE INN
Linton in Craven, BD23 5HJ •
01756 752210 • www.fountaineinnatlinton.co.uk
Opening hours: 11-11; 12-10.30 Sun

Upper Wharfedale

The beautiful Upper Wharfedale valley epitomises the Yorkshire Dales: a wide rural valley with limestone scars lining the valley sides and small villages clustered at regular intervals along the floor. It's walking country *par excellence* and deservedly popular. Likewise with its pubs, which are still fairly numerous; and, although they change hands from time to time, they offer fine fare and a widening variety of beers mainly from this proudly independent county. However, opening times can vary with the season, so I advise careful planning to establish what's open and when before setting out. The walk described here, like many others in this book, can be done in full or in part, in this case taken as two circuits with a connecting section. At the time of writing, the useful bus service up to Buckden is under threat of withdrawal on account of cuts to subsidies. If it's still in operation when you read this, it's a great way to get into and around the area.

WALK 4

▶ **Start/finish:** Kettlewell (Buckden for northern loop only)

▶ **Access:** Via Skipton or Ilkley using local bus services (www.prideofthedales.co.uk; www.dalesbus.org/874.html)

▶ **OS map:** Explorer OL30

▶ **Distance:** Southern loop 4.4 miles; connecting riverside path 2.2 miles; northern loop 4.9 miles. Total circuit 11.5 miles (18.5 km)

▶ **Key attractions:** Unspoilt valley with fine scenery; Dales Way riverside path

▶ **THE PUBS:** Buck Inn, Buckden; White Lion, Cray; George Inn, Hubberholme; Blue Bell Inn, Kettlewell. Try also: King's Head, Kettlewell; Fox & Hounds, Starbotton

▶ **Timing tips:** The complete circuit is a full day's walk, so a base in the area is recommended. Avoid Mondays and Tuesdays when the George Inn is not open at lunchtime. Check opening times at the White Lion carefully, since at the time of writing the pub was just about to re-open after a lengthy closure.

Kettlewell from the hillside

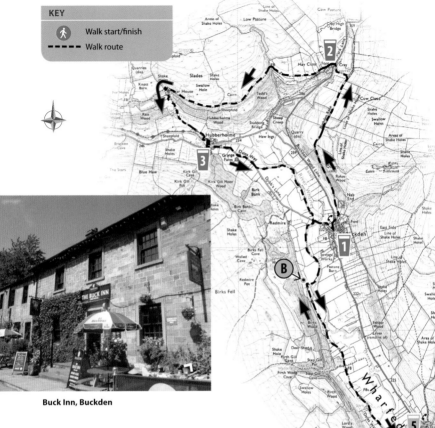

KEY

🚶 Walk start/finish

- - - - Walk route

Buck Inn, Buckden

🚶 My circuit begins at Kettlewell and as always, where possible, gets the bulk of the walking underway before the drinking starts. Kettlewell is, in common with the other settlements along beautiful Upper Wharfedale, a nucleated or clustered village with the houses very close together, usually where tributary streams or springs flow out to meet the Wharfe. From the bridge over the tributary in the village centre walk south (in the Burnsall and Skipton direction), passing the garage and tea room and over the Wharfe Bridge. Fifty yards or so later, bear onto the wide Land Rover track by the footpath sign, disregarding both the path hugging the river's edge and the less distinct left-hand track, which climbs up the limestone scar almost immediately. The wide

track follows the edge of the river flood plain, on the level at first but then starting to climb, steeply at one point, up the shoulder of limestone that separates Wharfedale from Littondale to the west. Quickly, a rewarding panorama opens up across the wide dale with its very distinctive 'U' profile typical of well-glaciated valleys. The River Wharfe occupying the valley today meanders freely across the valley floor. Higher up, the skyline across the valley includes the summits of both Great Whernside, above Kettlewell, and, further

Meanders on the Wharfe near Starbotton

The character of the path now changes dramatically as the route descends, as steeply as it climbed, through a small woodland towards the river. Take great care on this section as the path is stony, and in wet conditions potentially slippery. At the foot of the slope you'll come to the footbridge at Starbotton (**A** ⏱ **951745**). If you're on the southern circuit only, or intending

north – above Starbotton from this perspective – Buckden Pike, the highest point in the area at 702 metres (about 2,300 feet).

As the gradient eases, follow the Bridleway signs around an abandoned farmhouse and through a couple of fields to a gate, where the route to Starbotton leads through the gate and starts to descend. (Disregard a left-hand bridleway that bears off at this point over the ridge to Arncliffe in Littondale.)

to visit the Fox & Hounds at this point, then take the bridge and pick up the description below; otherwise, stay on the west bank of the river, taking the signed path to Buckden. Now it's two miles of easy and pleasant riverside walking below the wooded scars on your left. Watch out for the path turning at 90 degrees to the right off the forest track at (**B** ⏱ **939765**); but aside from this you can walk on autopilot until you are disgorged onto the usually quiet lane close to Buckden Bridge. Turn to the right, and it's a five-minute walk up into the pretty village of Buckden set around a small open green. This, incidentally, is also the place to start if you are undertaking only the northern loop.

The village pub is rather shyly hidden from immediate sight: walk a few yards south and the 🍴 **Buck Inn** comes into view, sitting in an elevated position with its own small green in front running up from the road. Once a coaching inn, it's a grand building that makes quite a statement in this small village; but like other rural pubs it has had its ups and downs, and periods of closure. New management in 2012 has revitalised the place from the beer to the bedrooms and lifted the Buck's

BLUE BELL, KETTLEWELL

The route enters Starbotton on a wooded and walled path

White Lion Inn, Cray

fortunes. The bar layout is sensibly divided between a stone-flagged area for the drinkers and a large comfortable lounge, itself divided into two distinct areas. Theakston's beers are joined by a surprisingly large selection of guests – sourced from near and far – which varies throughout the year but should always offer some choice. Food is varied and plentiful even if you just want a sandwich to fortify you for the onward journey. It's also an option to leave the Buck Inn for later and press straight on to Cray, perhaps stopping for a snack and/or hot drink in the little shop instead…

Retrace your last few steps to the northern end of village, beyond the green to the Town Head Barn Bunkhouse and car park. The onward path, which climbs the hillside, is visible as you approach. At the far end of the car park take the signed

Tour de France Grand Depart sign in Kettlewell

bridleway ('Cray High Bridge and Buckden Pike'). It's a steady uphill climb rewarded by magnificent views over the top end of the valley. Note the little hamlet of Hubberholme nestling in the valley below and, stretching away to the west, the narrower upstream continuation of the valley, now called Langstrothdale. Ignore paths leading off to the right and keep the wall hard on your left as the gradient eases and the path swings round more to the

right. Soon the tiny village of Cray appears below you: go through a gate, and look for another gate, in the wall left, with a modest signpost directing you steeply downhill to Cray village. This leads down to steps across the (usually very small) stream (it's unlikely that the stones will be covered but, if they are, you may have to continue north a bit to cross to the road), and conveniently out to the road right adjacent the **2** **White Lion Inn**. Newly re-opened after a period of closure this remote and attractive inn has been sympathetically updated to make the most of its idyllic location at the head of the valley. Nicely scrubbed-up stone floors, traditional dados and beamed ceilings, create an appealing arena in which to enjoy a selection of three Yorkshire ales (Black Sheep plus rotating guests). There's even a snug with its own log burner and comfy sofas. Note though that lunch service ends at 2.30pm.

Leaving the White Lion, the path carries on behind the pub. It's easy to follow (just ensure you ignore the left fork after 200 yards which leads back down to the road) and keeps almost on the level as the landscape falls away below you and you keep to a shelf on the horizontally layered carboniferous limestone that makes up this region. There

George Inn, Hubberholme

Pass the church and cross the bridge to reach the delightfully sited ▣ **George Inn**.

Access this lovely old white-washed traditional building via a pleasant sun-trap courtyard, possibly having been given the once-over from George, the owners' Jack Russell, who is far friendlier than most of the breed. The atmospheric interior has retained much character, including its small rooms lit by heavily mullioned stone windows, and an open fire. The beer range is better than ever with up to four cask ales on, including, at the time of writing, Black Sheep Bitter, Wharfedale Blonde and often a dark, rotating guest beer. Food is served until 2.30pm, but, as always, the advice is phone ahead to check.

It's a very hard pub to leave, but public transport is non-existent and it's two miles back to Buckden. Don't re-cross the bridge, but bear right onto quiet Dubbs Lane and walk for just over half a mile, passing Grange Farm before taking the signed path on the left beyond it; this takes you down to the

now follows a mile or so of the most pleasant walking through meadows with superb views down the length of Upper Wharfedale; and there are no navigational difficulties. Look out for Scar House just below you after a mile or so: it's the first habitation anywhere near the path. At this point you need to leave the level path by a signpost and head down towards the house; the right of way then follows the driveway steeply downhill, doubling back towards Hubberholme. Have mercy on those knees and take your time!

Langstrothdale and Hubberholme

"one of the smallest and pleasantest places in the world"

J.B. PRIESTLEY ON HUBBERHOLME

King's Head Kettlewell

riverside and offers a very nice stroll along the Wharfe back to Buckden, rejoining the lane almost opposite the path you used this morning to approach from Starbotton. Either retrace your outward route to Starbotton on the path, adding another two miles, or call in at the Buck Inn if you omitted it earlier. In the latter case, and if it's still running (see introduction), you may be able to pick up a bus down the valley instead of walking.

If the **5 Fox & Hounds** at Starbotton is open (it is closed 3–6pm each day) it's worth calling into this attractive whitewashed pub, which serves Timothy Taylor's Landlord and a changing guest.

The final leg of the circuit is the two-mile walk back to Kettlewell, this time keeping to the path on the east of the valley. Walk south towards the edge of this tiny village and, almost opposite the bridleway from the river footbridge, where a lane joins diagonally from the left, looking left you'll see the signed footpath striking up the hill to a step stile. Then it's a simple walk along the contour (keeping much lower than the outward path earlier in the day), negotiating a series of gates and stiles, until Kettlewell is reached. The short descent leads into the village at its north-eastern edge – bear left along the road passing the Youth Hostel and turn right at the well-stocked village store to reach the main road by the bridge, where two pubs face each other across the street. The **4 Blue Bell Inn**, an attractive building with

a character interior, is the oldest pub in the village and can get very busy in season. It has an interesting beer range: on tap expect at least four beers with a pronounced Yorkshire bias, with the likes of Wharfedale, Dales Brewing Co, and Hetton's Dark Horse brewery. The place is open all day and there's plenty of food. It also has several letting rooms if you need a place to stay in the village.

If you're game for another pub, you could try the **6 King's Head** on The Green, which has had a much-needed and tasteful makeover after lengthy closure and, although it specialises in food (and accommodation), drinkers also receive a friendly welcome. Among the three regulars on the handpumps is Dark Horse's excellent Hetton Pale Ale. To get to the King's Head, retrace your steps to the shop and turn right; or cross the river and bear left.

PUB INFORMATION

1 BUCK INN
Buckden, BD23 5JA •
01756 761401 • www.buckinnbuckden.co.uk
Opening hours: 12-3, 6-10.30 Mon-Thu (winter); 12-11 Mon-Thu (summer); 12-11 Fri & Sat; 12-10.30 Sun

2 WHITE LION INN
Cray, BD23 5JB •
01756 760262 • www.whitelioninncray.com
Opening hours: 12-10.30

3 GEORGE INN
Kirk Gill, Hubberholme, BD23 5JE •
01756 760223 • www.thegeorge-inn.co.uk
Opening hours: Summer: 4-10.30 Mon; closed Tue; 12-10.30 Wed-Sun
Winter: 6-10.30 Mon; closed Tue; 12-3, 6-10.30 Wed & Thu; 12-11 Fri & Sat; 12-5 Sun

4 BLUE BELL INN
Middle Lane, Kettlewell, BD23 5QX •
01756 760230 • www.bluebellkettlewell.co.uk
Opening hours: 12-10.30

Try also:

5 FOX & HOUNDS
Starbotton, BD23 5HY •
01756 760269 • www.foxandhoundsstarbotton.co.uk
Opening hours: 12-3, 6-11

6 KING'S HEAD
The Green, Kettlewell, BD23 5RD •
01756 761600 • www.thekingsheadkettlewell.co.uk
Opening hours: 11-11 (closed Mon in winter); 12-10.30 Sun

Two Georges & a Dragon: a Wensleydale three-village circular

Wensleydale is one of the widest and longest of the many Yorkshire Dales, and associated in many minds with its famous cheese, which was given a shot in the arm by TV duo Wallace & Gromit. Their patronage has reputedly led to a spike in production in the Hawes creamery. It's unlikely that Wallace's favourite cheese will recreate the economic diversity of the past when water-powered mills at valley villages like Gayle, Hawes, Thoralby, West Burton and Aysgarth were variously used to grind corn, produce textiles (wool, cotton, linen, silk and flax), generate electricity or saw wood, but the countryside today looks quietly prosperous nonetheless.

▶ **Start/finish:** Aysgarth, village green

▶ **Access:** The Little White Bus (www.littlewhitebus. co.uk) Wensleydale Voyager service has connections to/ from Richmond/Darlington or Garsdale Station on the Settle–Carlisle railway.

▶ **Distance:** 6.6 miles (10.6 km)

▶ **OS map:** Explorer OL30

▶ **Key attractions:** Aysgarth Falls; Castle Bolton (4 miles); West Burton village & Cauldron Falls; Wensleydale Railway (4 miles); Hawes (busy market town; 8 miles)

▶ **THE PUBS:** George, Thoralby; Fox & Hounds, West Burton; George & Dragon, Aysgarth. Try also: Aysgarth Falls Hotel

▶ **Timing tips:** Allow about 90 minutes to reach the George, which opens (at midday) for lunch except Mondays and Tuesdays (but only Fri-Sun in winter; check with pub if unsure). Lunch service at the Fox & Hounds ends at 2pm.

A Wensleydale field barn

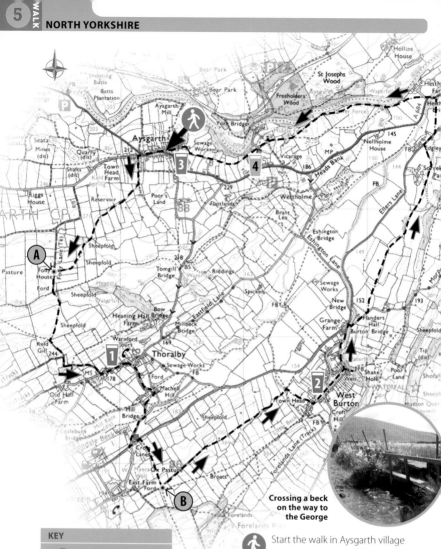

Crossing a beck on the way to the George

KEY

🚶 Walk start/finish

- - - - Walk route

The route described here starts and finishes at Aysgarth, deservedly known for its impressive sequence of waterfalls, and passes three of the old mills – sadly no longer working. Happily the pubs offer a far better range of beer than they ever did, as well as plenty of good food. They, like the villages, are interspersed at convenient intervals, and neither the terrain nor the navigation should prove overly difficult.

🚶 Start the walk in Aysgarth village close to the George & Dragon, which will later make a fitting finale to this circular walk. Head west along the village street, with its pleasant green – but only a pale imitation of West Burton's, which you'll visit later on. At the western end of Aysgarth village peel off to the left on the minor road ('Thornton Rust'), and, almost immediately, bear left on a footpath signed 'Tom Gill Bridge and Folly Lane'. Start ascending the hillside gently. Take care here, for once through the second field, and 50 yards short of a low barn, rights of way split. Head off to the right at 45 degrees towards a step stile in the wall, and, keeping more or less in the same south-westerly direction, cross several fields, passing a traditional field barn, then making for a large tree ahead. The path is not always well marked on the ground but you should be able to navigate via the stiles, mostly squeezer stiles protected by little wooden gates. You'll see a large three-window barn (passing to the left of it) and, beyond that, a pair of close-growing oaks. Just before, a reassuring signpost directs you to join Folly Lane, a walled green lane, at (**A** 🌣 995875).

George, Thoralby

Turn left (south) here, crossing a small stream over a plank footbridge. Climb up along the wall to a prominent waymark. You now enter a large field with no obvious features. Obey the broad direction of the sign, bearing away from the wall, and walk as far as the far boundary wall of the field. The way through is hidden in a small dip to the left of another pair of trees. As you top the brow of the rise, a marvellous view opens up before you, down into Bishopdale. Curiously this tributary valley of Wensleydale is considerably deeper than the latter (see box), so, after a modest climb from Aysgarth,

you're now presented with a long descent down into Thoralby below. Note also in the very rural scene the villages of Newbiggin and West Burton, which you can identify with the help of a map.

The route down into the village is now a simple case of following the good, wide track, steeply downhill, ignoring side paths, until you arrive at the road at the western end of the village. Thoralby is a quiet farming village on the northern side of the valley. Turn left and walk down to the 🍺 **George**. This small, stone village pub has benefited

The wide village green at West Burton

AYSGARTH FALLS & YORE MILL

Aysgarth Falls – really three cascades in rapid succession along the River Ure – are a product of the Ice Age. Several thousand years ago, the river valleys were deeply filled by ice, a far more powerful agent of erosion than mere water. Nearby Bishopdale was eroded deeper than Wensleydale and, once the ice melted, the River Ure had to drop a good distance to meet up with it, hence the falls, which drop in all some 100 feet (30 m). They have been a tourist attraction for more than 200 years: William Wordsworth and

his sister, Dorothy, visited; and J.M.W. Turner sketched them on his tour of the north in 1816. More recently they were used to provide a dramatic backdrop for a scene in the film *Robin Hood, Prince of Thieves* (1991). By the bridge below the church, Yore Mill is a four-storey listed building, built in 1784, and an early example of rural industrialisation. The mill continued in use well into the 20th century, though water turbines replaced the wheels for the last years of its working life until it ceased flour production in 1959.

The Ure at Aysgarth

from enthusiastic licensees who offer a welcome, good food and three changing beers, primarily from local brewers. The interior has been smartened up and the two rooms joined through, but there is still some character including an impressive fireplace at the western end. It's an obvious port of call for lunch unless you're very early in arriving, since the next pub is another couple of miles on.

Continue from the George along the village street and turn right before the pretty village green heading down towards the river. The road is quiet, but in consultation with your map you can avoid a couple of bends by bearing left near the foot of the hill and right along a path towards Thoralby Mill, rejoining the road just before the bridge over the Bishopdale Beck. The old corn mill is defunct now, converted into flats. Follow the road to the right ('Kettlewell') at the junction and head up to the next junction, with the B6160, by a bunk barn. Here, watching out for traffic, turn left for a few yards and take the signed path opposite heading to the right (south) across a couple of fields. You'll join a shady, fenced green lane via a stile (**B** 🔵 004853). Now, simply turn to your left and follow this pleasant if stony track

until it disgorges into a field close to a stone barn. Continue on the same bearing through fields via a combination of stiles and gates. The track in the grass is usually distinct enough to follow through this very quiet and rural landscape, but keep an eye on the map as you negotiate this half a mile or so. Look out for Bolton Castle in the distance straight ahead. Just after you cross a tiny stream on a stone bridge, look for a squeezer stile on the right, about 10 yards beyond. Turn uphill here keeping to the right of the field barn and emerge on the road at the top of West Burton village.

West Burton, dominated by its large village green, is considered to be one of the most beautiful villages in the Yorkshire Dales. Villages with greens are found throughout the country but are particularly common in areas where, in the past, defence was a prime consideration. Animals would often be herded onto the green for protection. As you walk down into the village, the houses line the green on each side of the slope. In some places buildings have encroached onto the green, but it still remains extensive. Occupying an enviable location looking out across the green and close to the unusual village 'cross' and stocks stands the **2** **Fox & Hounds**. A pretty, traditional, whitewashed building, it looks bigger on the outside than in, but there is a separate dining room as well as the traditional low-beamed bar with its imposing stone fireplace. In good weather you may well elect to sit outside and watch the world not going by very quickly. Black Sheep Bitter is available alongside Theakston and John Smith's; and a lunch menu is available, if you get there on time. Evening meals are also served from 6pm.

As you depart from the Fox & Hounds, it's worth making the short detour to see the Cauldron Falls at the lower end of the village, one of the waterfalls drawn by J.M.W. Turner during his tour of the north of England in 1816. Make your way across from the pub to the cottages across the green and walk down to the bottom by the old mill, now a private house. The falls are yards away just beyond a pretty footbridge and an information board. The falls, where the little Walden Beck flows down over a series of limestone steps, is a charming little spot and it's easy to see what attracted Turner.

Leave West Burton on the road at the lower end of the village, taking care on the narrow stretch, passing some more attractive houses; just as the road meets the B6160, bear right on a small lane over a pretty stone bridge, named after the village. The significant building on the left is Flanders Hall, a large Georgian country house dating from circa 1780, with some attractive architectural features. The accompanying stable block is equally appealing. About 150 yards beyond the hall, on the bend, take the clearly signed path ('Edgeley 1 mile'). Once again, it's a question of following the worn grass through the meadows, looking for the stiles. Just after crossing a small stream and entering a larger field, the path drops a little to the left, down a bank (wooden signpost at foot) towards a large house, Sorrelsykes, ahead, which from this elevation looks more like a Palladian mansion. The original owners were in all probability eccentric since they also had constructed a series of follies on the hillside to your right, not readily visible from the path. You can find out more about the Sorrelsykes follies on the internet.

Keep the house on your left, and note that the farm track to the road is not the right of way. Bear off to the left of it, keeping a big sycamore tree on your right, reaching the road at the end of the line of houses on the lane ahead, by a sign. Walk down the road

The gently rolling Wensleydale landscape

Fox & Hounds, West Burton

a short way bearing off to the left in about 100 yards by rusty metal gates and follow the clear path through the field towards the trees. The last section down to the busy A684 takes you through the little woodland for a short distance. Note the now rare old AA call box on the road to the right and, once more, very clear views of Bolton Castle ahead. The 100 yards or thereabouts on the main road need great care: there is no footpath and the road bends awkwardly to cross the river. Once safely across a clear path is signed across the meadow on the corner of the entrance lane to Hestholme Farm. Already the roar of the waters as they plunge down Aysgarth Falls is competing with the noise of the traffic. Now it's a case of following this path, but disappointingly the riverside vegetation is quite thick and clear sightings of the river here are few and far between.

Keep on the path as it actually veers away from the riverside to an extent and climbs up into the churchyard of the parish church of St Andrew. Rebuilt in 1536 and restored in 1866, this distinctive listed building has an extensive churchyard of about four acres. Inside the church are fittings and features that were saved by the monks from Jervaulx Abbey during the Dissolution of the Monasteries. These include the great Rood Screen and the Abbot's Stall. Part of an ancient Saxon cross was sadly stolen in 1996.

From the churchyard the path meets the road down to the falls and the old mill, though there is a safer and more direct path steeply down from the far side of the churchyard straight down to the river, should you wish to take in the detour.

From the church, the path crosses the road and through the bottom of a campsite (see the reference to Aysgarth Falls Hotel, below) and is then followed easily through a series of fields to arrive in the village by the **3 George & Dragon**. This is a venerable old coaching inn, now listed, with at its core a cosy wood-panelled bar room with an open fire. On the bar you can expect up to five real ales including Black Sheep Best Bitter and one or two from the nearby Yorkshire Dales brewery. There is a good evening menu served 6–8.30pm, if you're planning to eat here; accommodation is offered too.

If you want to try another pub, then just to the east on the main road (at the junction of the lane down to the falls) is the **4 Aysgarth Falls Hotel**, now much improved for the ale drinker with up to five cask ales from local and regional brewers. The pub also owns the good-value campsite, which the route crossed on the way into the village.

PUB INFORMATION

1 GEORGE
Thoralby, DL8 3SU •
01969 663256 • www.thegeorgeinnthoralby.com
Opening hours: 6.30-11 Mon-Thu; 12-2, 6.30-11 Fri-Sun

2 FOX & HOUNDS
West Burton, DL8 4JY •
01969 663111 • www.foxandhoundswestburton.co.uk
Opening hours: 9am-12.30am

3 GEORGE & DRAGON
Aysgarth, DL8 3AD •
01969 663358 • www.georgeanddragonaysgarth.co.uk
Opening hours: 11-midnight

Try also:

4 AYSGARTH FALLS HOTEL
Aysgarth, DL8 3SR •
01969 663228 • www.aysgarthfallshotel.com
Opening hours: 11.30-11

A Swaledale classic: from Muker to Keld

This well-known and deservedly popular walk encircles Kisdon Hill at the furthest end of the valley that Alfred Wainwright, the great walker and author, considered to be the finest of the Dales – a view with which I have no issue. Keld's pub, the Cat Hole Inn, closed its doors in 1954 after being bought by a temperance campaign group (boo!), but happily the hamlet is no longer dry since the former Youth Hostel has now been transformed into the comfortable Keld Lodge, which offers real ale as well as good food and hospitality. The route finishes at the ever-popular little Farmers Arms at Muker, but it's perfectly possible to start this circuit at either place. Navigation is as easy as the landscape is attractive.

▸ **Start/finish:** Muker, Farmers Arms, or Keld

▸ **Access:** Via Richmond and Reeth with Swaledale Shuttle buses 30/32 (www.littlewhitebus.co.uk))

▸ **OS map:** Explorer OL30

▸ **Distance:** 6 miles (3.75 km)

▸ **Key attractions:** Superb scenery and views; waterfalls in Keld; industrial archaeology (lead mines and smelters); ruins of Crackpot Hall

▸ **THE PUBS:** Keld Lodge, Keld; Farmers Arms, Muker

▸ **Timing tips:** Whichever village you start from, allow a couple of hours to reach the first pub. Food service at lunchtimes is until 2.30pm.

Muker nestling in the Swaledale landscape

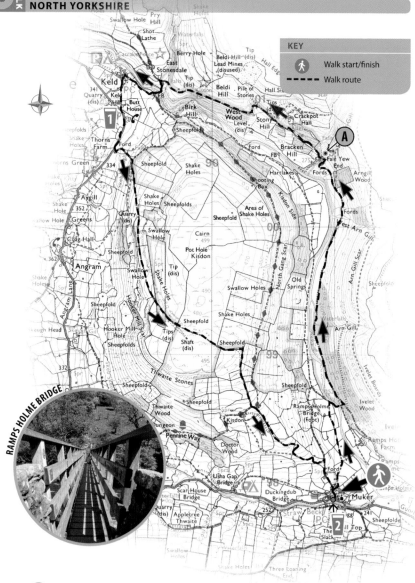

KEY

🚶 Walk start/finish

- - - - Walk route

The centre of Muker is very compact. If you are arriving by car, the car park is just east of the village; or the Little White Bus will deposit you right outside the pub. Walk a few yards back, admiring the Flemish-style former Literary Institute before heading up the lane to the left, passing the public hall and the church; passing Corner Cottage and heading up past the red post box on your left, you'll see the waymarks ('Keld and Gunnerside') that lead you out of the village on the *bon chemin*. Follow the clear path through several fields until you near the River Swale, whence turn right to cross it on the Ramps Holme Bridge. Turn left following the signpost for Keld. It's really a simple walk now all the way to Keld, and you can admire the landscape without contending with navigational difficulties.

Crackpot Hall

upstream suggest it is still modifying that course even today. The valley shape here, with its wide floor flanked by steep sides, is typical of glaciated valleys, although this one has probably been caused by a large meltwater stream after that last glaciation.

Swaledale and its tributary valleys probably have more evidence of past lead mining than any other of the Yorkshire Dales, and the rich veins of lead ore have been exploited from at least Roman times. You can see evidence of this close up as you use the footbridge to cross the Swinner Gill (Ⓐ 🧭 909005). Today a picturesque ruin, the Beldi Hill smelter was built here in the late 18th century and made use of the power of the gill at this point. The track climbs uphill beyond Swinner Gill, and looking back you should be ale to spot more

The isolated Kisdon Hill stands on the far bank of the river: Kisdon Hill is unusual in that it has valleys running either side of it and has no connecting ridges to any other high ground. This is attributed to the diversion of the course of the River Swale during the last glaciation, when moraine (glacial debris) blocked the original course and forced the river to carve a new path north of the hill. The various waterfalls further

The path skirts the side of Kisdon Hill

East Beck Force, Keld

leaved woodland. Ahead of you now the little village of Keld comes into view. Keld is aptly named from the Norse *kelda* (a spring), whilst nearby Thwaite (a clearing) and Muker (the narrow acre) itself are also Norse in origin. Most of the little village is clustered around a tiny green near the river, but the large building up on the left is Keld Lodge, which started life as a shooting lodge before becoming a youth hostel and, now, your first refreshment stop on the route. It's still a half-mile away yet, though.

Descend to cross East Gill on a bridge, just beyond which the path forks – to the right, the Pennine Way continues north towards the lonely Tan Hill Inn four miles away. You turn left, passing East Gill Force and descending to cross the Swale on a footbridge, climbing up to another path junction. Here, leave the Pennine Way again and head right, a short walk up into the lower part of the village, passing the church. There's a very well-stocked tea room with cakes etc. at Park Lodge straight ahead, but if it's midday you may well prefer to head uphill, passing the United Reformed Church (this area was a bastion of non-conformism) and the little Keld Countryside and Heritage centre. This information centre occupies the former horse stables and coach room in the Literary Institute Building; it was restored and opened to the public (free admission) in 2011. Continue uphill to join the B6270 road. The three-storied building just to the right of the junction is 🛏 **Keld Lodge**, our first stop of the day.

Keld is a place well used to accommodating people passing through: it's the crossing point of two of our best-loved long-distance paths, the Pennine Way and Wainwright's Coast to Coast path. So it's maybe no surprise, then, that after the YHA closed the Keld hostel and new owners spent a small fortune refurbishing the rather neglected building,

ruins: these are of Crackpot Hall, close to the track (a path doubles back to it if you wish to take a closer look). The name is a derivation from Norse and refers to crows and potholes rather than mad humans! However, it was visited by Ella Pontefract, the famous Yorkshire social historian, in the 1930s and she wrote of a 'wild' four-year-old child living here by the name of Alice; but Alice and her family must have moved out by around 1951 as the building had become unsafe owing to mining subsidence.

The path descends once again, and below you the sound of Kisdon Force is audible. The largest of four local 'forces' (from the Norse *foss*, a waterfall), these falls drop 10 metres (33 feet) over two cascades but are hidden, especially in summer, by mixed broad-

Keld Lodge

turn back down the hill, is the old Cat Hole Inn, now a private house. Hardly 200 yards further along, a bridleway bears off to your left towards a stone barn. Drop steeply down to ford the stream, whereafter the wide track, walled in places, pulls its way up the side of Kisdon Hill. This path is called the Corpse Road. Like many similar old roads the length and breadth of the country it was used to carry coffins to the nearest consecrated ground (in this case, originally, Grinton near Reeth,

it has become a very popular place to stay. Happily Keld Lodge also has a small public bar, and Black Sheep Bitter is available on handpump, usually with a small selection of bottles from the same brewery.

On leaving Keld Lodge, bear right and follow the road towards the hamlet of Angram. The last building on the left, just beyond the

before the first chapel of ease was built in Muker in 1580). In good weather the next mile or so is a very pleasant easy walk with great views. The big flat-topped hill across to your right is Great Shunner Fell, and at about 2,350 ft (716 metres) the highest summit so far for walkers heading north on the Pennine Way. The road crossing into Wensleydale

Beldi Hill has evidence of former lead mining

"a sundial records the hours but time is measured in centuries at Keld"

ALFRED WAINWRIGHT, *A COAST TO COAST WALK*

Farmers Arms, Muker

The Swale near Kisdon Force

on the shoulder of the hill is the Buttertubs pass, one of the longer ascents (not quite of Alpine severity, however) during the 2014 Yorkshire section of the Tour de France.

Rounding the shoulder of Kisdon Hill a fine view eastwards down Swaledale appears, with the village of Muker coming into view once more below. There's one sharp right turn before the real descent begins: it's steep in places and requires a little care with your feet, although, of course, the path itself is easy to follow. You cross the Pennine Way once again as you cover this last mile or so down to the village, and the path leads right into the centre and therefore, of course, to the **2** **Farmers Arms**. This homely little Dales pub has changed little in the 30-odd years I have known it: half of the small public space is flagged with local stone, so walkers and their boots are always welcome; and, whilst good food is served, the pub's website emphasises, correctly, that it's not a gastro pub and it doesn't allow any prior booking of tables, a policy I wish more pubs would follow. The place is currently up for sale, but I doubt if the new owners would dare change this too much – it works very well as it is.

One thing that *has* altered, favourably, is the beer range, which, with up to five ales on tap, is better than ever. Black Sheep Bitter and Theakston's Old Peculier retain a link with the past favourites, whilst the local Yorkshire Dales brewery supplies a couple, including the house beer. Expect a rotating guest too. In warm weather the outside seats are very popular and you can see just about everything that's going on in this pleasant little village without letting go of your pint.

Armed with a map, keen walkers could extend their day with a saunter down the valley via a good path to the King's Head at Gunnerside – otherwise the Farmers Arms is open all day for your enjoyment!

PUB INFORMATION

1 **KELD LODGE**
Keld, DL11 6LL •
01748 886259 • www.keldlodge.com
Opening hours: 10-10

2 **FARMERS ARMS**
Muker, DL11 6QG •
01748 886297 • www.farmersarmsmuker.co.uk
Opening hours: 11.30-midnight (11 Mon);
11.30-11 Sun

Knaresborough to Harrogate via the Nidd Gorge

This scenic stroll between two of North Yorkshire's most attractive towns is easier than the distance suggests, and offers plenty of excellent drinking opportunities in each. Whilst Harrogate's appeal as a spa town is well known, smaller Knaresborough nestling around its castle ruins occupies a commanding site overlooking the River Nidd and its picturesque railway viaduct, reached by a steep descent. A wooded gorge leads to a CAMRA heritage pub whence one can return to Knaresborough or continue, to take in Harrogate on the same day. A street plan of Harrogate (free in the Tourist Office) is a helpful extra.

▶ **Start:** Knaresborough, Market Place

▶ **Finish:** Knaresborough or Harrogate

▶ **Access:** Good rail links via York or Leeds

▶ **Distance:** Knaresborough to Harrogate town centre 7 miles (11.2 km)

▶ **OS map:** Explorer 289

▶ **Key attractions:** Knaresborough Castle and grounds; Knaresborough's *trompe l'oeil* windows; Conyngham Hall grounds; Nidd Gorge Trail; Harrogate architecture and spa with Turkish baths

▶ **THE PUBS:** Gardeners Arms, Bilton; Swan on the Stray, Winter Gardens, Hales Bar, Harrogate Tap, all Harrogate; Blind Jack's, Cross Keys Inn, Half Moon, all Knaresborough. Try also: 10 Devonshire Place, Major Tom's Social, Blues Café Bar, all Harrogate.

▶ **Timing tip:** The Gardeners Arms is about 70–80 minutes' walk from Knaresborough and opens at midday.

Knaresborough and the Nidd

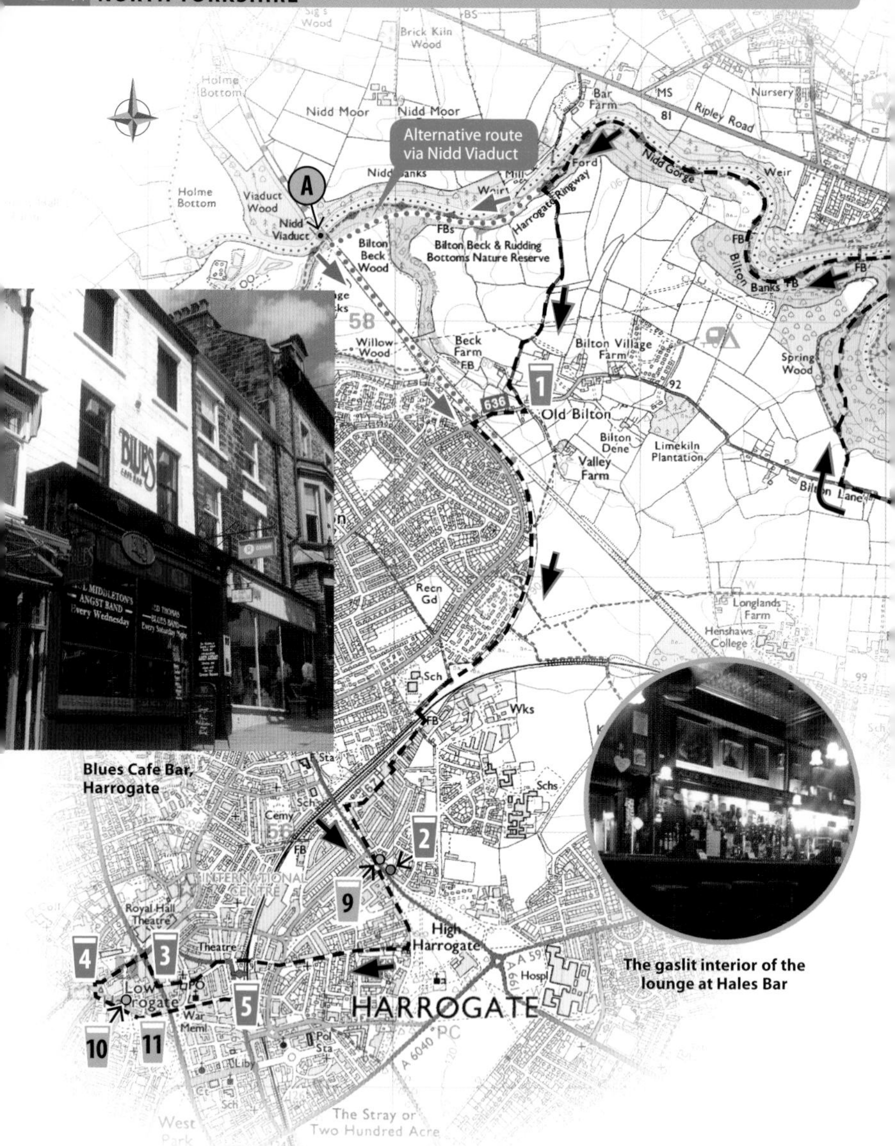

Alternative route via Nidd Viaduct

A

Blues Cafe Bar, Harrogate

1

2

9

4 **3**

5

10 **11**

HARROGATE

High Harrogate

The gaslit interior of the lounge at Hales Bar

Knaresborough's little market place is a good spot to get the walk underway. It's about a five-minute uphill walk from the railway station via Kirkgate, and close to the castle grounds, which also afford the best angle of the town's signature view: the rail viaduct spanning the River Nidd. If you've seen it all before, you can also join the route described by turning right (downhill) out of the station by the Mitre Inn.

The best way down to the river is taking the path (signed to 'Waterside and Boating') close by the castle grounds entrance (and public conveniences) at Castle Yard. Bear left into Bebra Gardens before the path runs out and find the onward steps at the far side of the paddling pool. This will bring you out on Waterside, the quiet lane running along the riverside. Turn right and walk towards the viaduct. An elegant structure, it stands 78 feet

KEY

🚶 Walk start

- - - - Walk route

•••••• Alternative route

Entrance to the Swan on the Stray

KNARESBOROUGH

high above the water, and was opened in 1851, three years after its predecessor collapsed just before completion. Pass the old Indigo Mill, where a blue plaque indicates that this was the site of a manorial corn mill going back a millennium. The pretty riverside lane is flanked with old houses and a defunct brewery, although in fact, Knaresborough does once again have a brewery, Roosters, which is on the industrial estate, in keeping with the modern trend.

Reach the road bridge by the World's End pub and turn left to cross the river, then immediately right on Beryl Burton's Cycleway. Beryl (1937–1996), a Yorkshire woman of course, dominated UK women's cycling but also won half a dozen world titles, so it's fitting that this popular (and recently resurfaced) cycle route should bear her name.

Head into the woodland and follow this cycle path for about a mile, disregarding

other paths, over a couple of cattle grids and steadily uphill passing Bilton Hall on the right. Keep ahead at a junction of paths, and pass a house on your left where the path shifts slightly to the right. Now look out for a metal gate, covered in homemade admonitions, to a path on the right. This is the right of way (on foot only, as is made very clear to you!), which you now take – if you're lucky, you may see a kestrel, as I did, hunting in the field to the left. It's a good clear path, which enters the woodland. Keep ahead, bearing slightly to the right at a locked gate, where the track starts to descend, steeply in places, to the river below.

The heavily wooded Nidd Gorge – a very popular walk but once difficult of access especially after heavy rain – is now, thanks to improvement work, much more comfortable to navigate; although, as you traverse the mile or so along the gorge (keeping close

THE NIDD GORGE

Like many of the gorges in North Yorkshire, Nidd Gorge is a product of the last ice age when the Devensian ice sheet moved south in what is now the Vale of York. A combination of the ice sheet with sands and gravels pushed along at the margins of the ice forced the ancestor of the River Nidd further south and east from its earlier course to the north of modern Knaresborough, until the lake impounded by the ice found the easiest way through the lowest and softest rocks in the Permian and Carboniferous rocks, which now make up the Nidd Gorge. Geology enthusiasts can find out much more at: http://nora.nerc.ac.uk/4567/1/OR08044.pdf

The Nidd Gorge from the viaduct

to the river on the main path), you'll need to take care since many of the duckboards that have been put in to help you cross the muddiest sections can themselves get pretty slippery now that the wire covering is being worn away in places. That aside, it's a very pleasant walk.

Watch out after a mile or so for the point at which you should leave the river path. At an open wooden gateway, look out for a blue bridleway waymark on the post. A good, wide, earthen path strikes uphill. Take this path, which levels off after the initial rise. You'll arrive at a three-way fingerboard.

If you want to tackle the detour to take in the Nidd viaduct upstream (see box on p55), then bear right ('Batchelor Gardens') and follow the instructions in the box. Otherwise, follow the route pointing to the Gardeners Arms. This is one of those paths that is much more interesting than it looks on the map: a bosky sunken path with views out of the trees across the plateau beyond. Near the end join the tarmac driveway of a house, emerging on the quiet road right by the 🍺 **Gardeners Arms**. A splendid old 18th-century house, this listed building now has several rooms in pub use; but the most impressive and probably the oldest is the fine old taproom (front left), with an ancient fireplace and old bench seating. The lounge, on the other side of the flagged central corridor, is another good room in this well-proportioned gritstone building. It's a Samuel Smith house with Old Brewery Bitter the only real ale, but a must-see and an important entry in CAMRA's *Yorkshire's Real Heritage Pubs*.

When you leave the Gardeners Arms, you can choose to head back to Knaresborough without taking in Harrogate: there are several good options for pub visits in Knaresborough on its own. If you do decide to do this, it's a simple walk: just bear left on the lane out of the pub and continue on this quiet tarred lane, passing Bilton Farm holiday park, and in less than a mile rejoining the outward route by the memorable metal gate. Now retrace your outward route to the road bridge at Knaresborough and remember to bear left into Waterside by the World's End before consulting the Knaresborough entries later in this section.

To continue, instead, towards Harrogate, turn right from the Gardeners Arms and walk down the road to the old railway track (which you have recently left if you tackled the Nidd viaduct option). Turn onto this heading left, and it's a 15-minute walk along this aptly named 'Greenway' as it curves around the edge of suburban Harrogate. The Knaresborough railway joins from your left. Shortly afterwards, with school grounds

Inside the Gardeners Arms, Bilton

on the right, fork left to cross the railway bridge. Now, bear left on Grove Park Avenue to follow the railway towards an industrial building ahead, where you bear left, then follow round to the right (Grove Park Terrace) and walk up to join the A59, the main road. Now turn left along curiously named Dragon View and, shortly, close to the pelican crossing, you'll find the **2 Swan on the Stray**. Formerly known as the Black Swan (and with a handsome bas-relief swan above the door to prove it), this pub was given a modern makeover some five

Wetherspoons' sumptuous Winter Gardens

years back. It offers a very good range of up to eight real ales, from Yorkshire and beyond, complemented by a choice of foreign beer (on draught and in bottle) and a real cider. If it's that time of day by now (and it probably is), there's a good range of bar meals as well in this *Good Beer Guide* regular.

For the onward route walk back a few yards to cross the road at the crossing. However, depending upon the time of day, the old Devonshire Arms adjacent, now known as **9 10 Devonshire Place**, is well worth a visit if you have the stamina: it doesn't open until 3pm except at weekends (hence not a full entry here), but it has a changing, extensive and imaginative beer list on cask and key keg, housed in an interesting building that has been sympathetically refurbished.

Once across the road, head to the left by the pleasant avenue of trees along Regent Parade at the edge of the widening green known as the Stray. Shortly after crossing a cycle route, head down the narrow path, Walkers Passage, on the right by 29 Park Parade. Cross the road at the end straight into Kingsway, in turn crossing

into Bower Street, at the bottom of which a subway leads under the railway and disgorges you into Harrogate's town centre.

"the queerest place with the strangest people in it"

CHARLES DICKENS ON HARROGATE, 1858

Straight ahead, fork left into pedestrianised Oxford Street by the distinctive turret. Keep straight ahead until you reach Parliament Street (the A61), and turn right. (An optional extra here if you have the time and energy is, instead, to continue across into The Ginnel, where a short walk down is **10 Major Tom's Social**. It's an unusual café bar-cum-pizzeria-cum-art gallery, which takes its beers seriously. Expect four changing beers from Roosters and smaller breweries alongside a worthwhile range of bottles. Then return to Parliament Street.)

You won't miss the **3 Winter Gardens** a few yards north on Parliament Street. Whatever your views about JD Wetherspoon pubs, it's undeniably another superb conversion by JDW, this one from part of the magnificent Royal Baths complex in 2002. The spacious interior is reached via a sweeping double stone staircase. As usual there's plenty of choice on the beer front alongside the usual reliable Wetherspoons food fare.

Time and space precludes any attempt to do justice to the array of noteworthy buildings and attractions in central Harrogate, but on leaving the Winter Gardens and taking the first left north (Crescent Road) on Parliament Street you reach the Tourist Office, where you can take advice and pick up a free street map if you want a sightseeing break.

The punishing pub itinerary continues further down Crescent Road on the right, in the shape of **4 Hales Bar**. Occupying a prominent corner site, Harrogate's oldest pub (also featured in *Yorkshire's Real Heritage Pubs* for its historic interior) has an impressive Victorian bar with original gas lighting. There are six handpumps, with a house beer (by Daleside), Draught Bass (rare these days) and Timothy Taylor's Landlord, along with two changing beers, all supported by a food menu.

Across the road from Hales Bar, tree-lined Crown Place cuts up past the Pump Room Museum to Royal Parade. Cross and bear left passing the Old Bell Tavern before aiming across the roundabout on the same trajectory into classy Montpellier Hill, following the row of shops on the left up the hill onto Montpellier Parade. Another 'try also' possibility here is the **11 Blues Café Bar** with its picture windows looking out onto the green. Four rotating guest beers are offered, sourced from far and wide.

Colourful entrance to Major Tom's Social in Harrogate

NIDD VIADUCT ALTERNATIVE ROUTE

If you continue on the river towards the viaduct, follow the river path, which makes its way back down towards water level. Once again take care to leave the path at the right place: there's no direct link from the riverside path at the viaduct to the old railway path that crosses it above at (**A** 🕲 306584). Instead, in a few minutes cross a small stream on a little footbridge. The riverside path is signed off to the right. Here, bear left once across the footbridge, on an unsigned but very clear path that climbs up out of the trees to the edge of field. Here, keep right and hug the woodland margin (and gorge below) until you join the old Pateley Bridge railway, now

The woodland path through the Nidd Gorge

a Sustrans cycle and walking trail, part of the Nidderdale Greenway. The viaduct is of course immediately to your right, and before heading off, in the other direction, it's

worth a few steps to enjoy the view from the top. A 10-minute walk back along the trail brings you to a road, and here, turn left again to reach the Gardeners Arms in no time.

Just beyond is Betty's famous (and very expensive) tea room, and on the main road, the big war memorial. From here, it's a short walk across the main road and east via Cambridge Street and the Victoria Shopperama to Harrogate Station. Here, the **5** **Harrogate Tap** is yet another in Yorkshire's large and growing inventory of station bars. The solid but unpretentious building has been brought back to life with smart wood panelling and tiled floors, but the star is the range of real ales, surely one of the widest in town, with 11 to choose from as well as a draught cider (check website for current offerings). The other advantage is that you can time your exit for the train back to Knaresborough (if that's your intention) to perfection. If you're allergic to trains, the bus station is but a stone's throw away as well.

Once back in Knaresborough, make your way up into the Market Place once more and head for the town's most well-known pub, **6** **Blind Jack's**. It's named after the amazing John Metcalf (1717–1810), who could and did turn his hand to almost anything

but emerged as one of the country's earliest professional road builders, despite being blind from birth. It's a welcoming and cosy multi-roomed pub with a great range of nine, mostly changing beers, served up in fine condition as the 20-year run in the *Good Beer Guide* testifies. You can also view two so-called '*trompe l'oeil*' painted windows on the front elevation of the pub. There are several more around the town centre.

From Blind Jack's, a very short walk to your right and down Castlegate leads to the **7** **Cross Keys Inn**, a traditional local with stone-flagged floors, now in the growing portfolio of the ambitious Ossett brewery. Most of the half dozen ales here are of course from Ossett, so expect a strong emphasis on ultra-light beers; though the guests often include a darker beer.

The final pub is an easy downhill stroll to the river, fitting for a marathon like this (but you do have to get back afterwards!). Turn right out of the Cross Keys and right again when you reach the T-junction. Now follow the road right down to the river by the lower bridge, a pleasant spot when the traffic dies down in the evening. On the corner is the **8** **Half Moon**. New owners have made a lovely job of restoring this little pub inside and out (where they have removed the rendering and rather ridiculous shutters to reveal the red brickwork once again). Real fires keep the place warm in winter and, if you're here on Boxing Day, a team from the Half Moon takes on rivals from the Mother Shipton Inn just across the river in an annual tug-of-war, which has been a fixture for almost 50 years. Four handpumps dispense a varying range of Yorkshire beers, usually including one from nearby Rooster's. Food is in the form of meat and cheese platters.

If you're heading back to the station, the best bet is via Waterside, the riverside lane opposite the pub. The bus station is up the hill, I'm afraid!

Blind Jack's in Knaresborough market place

PUB INFORMATION

1 **GARDENERS ARMS**
Bilton Lane, Bilton, HG1 4DH
01423 506051
Opening hours: 12-11

2 **SWAN ON THE STRAY**
17 Devonshire Place, Harrogate, HG1 4AA
01423 524587
Opening hours: 11-11; 12-10.30 Sun

3 **WINTER GARDENS**
4 Royal Baths, Harrogate, HG1 2RR
01423 8770107
Opening hours: 7-midnight (1am Thu; 2am Fri & Sat)

4 **HALES BAR**
1-3 Crescent Road, Harrogate, HG1 2RS
01423 725570
www.halesbar.co.uk
Opening hours: 12-midnight (1am Thu-Sat); 12-11.30 Sun

5 **HARROGATE TAP**
Station Parade, Harrogate, HG1 1TE
01423 501644 • www.harrogatetap.co.uk
Opening hours: 11-11; 10-midnight Fri & Sat

6 **BLIND JACK'S**
19 Market Place, Knaresborough, HG5 8AL
01423 869148
Opening hours: 4 (3 Fri; 12 Sat)-11; 12-10.30 Sun

7 **CROSS KEYS INN**
17 Cheapside, Knaresborough, HG5 8AX
01423 863562
Opening hours: 12 (4 Mon & Tue)-11; 12-midnight Fri & Sat

8 **HALF MOON**
1 Abbey Road, Knaresborough, HG5 8HY
014213 313461
Opening hours: 5 (12 Sat)-11; 12-10.30 Sun

Try also:

9 **10 DEVONSHIRE PLACE**
The Ginnel, Harrogate, HG1 2RB
01423 566591
www.10devonshireplace.com
Opening hours: 13 (12 Sat & Sun)-midnight

10 **MAJOR TOM'S SOCIAL**
The Ginnel, Harrogate, HG1 2RB
01423 566984
www.majortomssocial.co.uk
Opening hours: 11-11.30 (1am Fri & Sat)

11 **BLUES CAFÉ BAR**
4 Montpellier Parade, Harrogate, HG1 2TJ
01423 566881
www.bluesbar.co.uk
Opening hours: 10-1am Mon-Sat; 12-12.30am Sun

Castleton & Danby

Careful pre-planning is needed to get the most from this rewarding walk taking in a round of two of the best ridges (or Riggs) projecting into pretty Eskdale, especially if you're using public transport. Despite quite a bit of (albeit mostly quiet) road walking, the route takes in some excellent scenery, but make no mistake, the full round is a long one and recommended only for fit walkers who don't mind a good yomp before the first pub. There's a shorter alternative which omits the airy plateau of Danby Moor. The route climbs to 1000' on the ridges with great views, but unless you're an experienced walker the route is not recommended in poor visibility, and navigation needs care in places. Take food and drink as the first pub is several miles into the walk. The three pubs on the round are all *Good Beer Guide* regulars so expect your ale to be well-kept and with a good choice. Keep an eye on the time as the Duke of Wellington is closed between 2.30 and 7 during the week.

▶ **Start/finish:** Castleton Moor railway station

▶ **Access:** Rail services (4 a day) from Whitby and Middlesbrough

▶ **Distance:** 9.5 miles (15.3 km) for full circuit. 6.4 miles (10.3km) for shorter circuit

▶ **OS maps:** Explorer OL26, Explorer OL27

▶ **Key attractions:** Heather moorlands on Castleton & Danby Riggs; North York Moors visitor centre, Danby village; St Hilda's church; Danby Agricultural Show (August)

▶ **PUBS:** Duke of Wellington, Danby; Downe Arms, Eskdale Inn, both Castleton

▶ **Timing tips:** If using the rail service from Whitby or Middlesbrough check timetable carefully. The 8.50 train from Whitby followed by a steady speed should allow you to catch the 2.50 pm return train from Castleton Moor. Avoid Mondays if you want to get into all the pubs!

Moorland heather in Westerdale

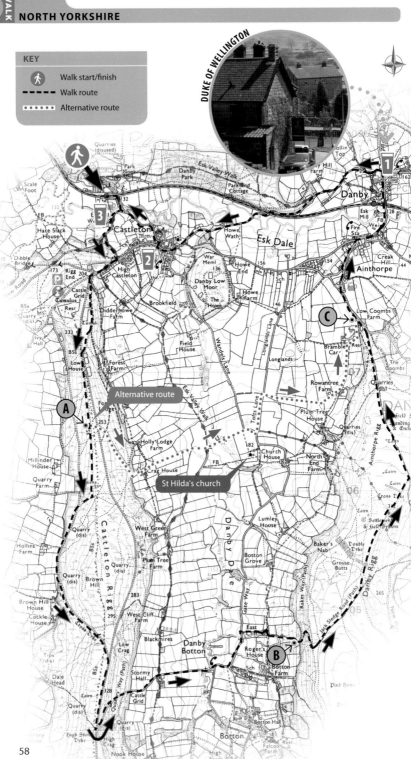

DUKE OF WELLINGTON

KEY

🚶 Walk start/finish

- - - - Walk route

•••••• Alternative route

Alternative route

St Hilda's church

From Castleton Moor station walk down to the road and turn under the bridge, passing the Eskdale Inn. Cross the river and follow the Esk Valley Walk sign at the road junction. As the road starts to climb, look out for a waymark and path leading uphill to the left. Take this path which climbs fairly steeply up towards the village street at the top of the brae. When you reach this, bear right and maybe use the welcome seats a little further along to gather your breath and admire the view.

At the end of the village disregard further Esk Valley Walk signs, and instead follow the wall round to the left hand fork (promising sheep for 14 miles!?) at the three-road junction. The bracken on the footpath by the five bar gate just beyond is very dense in summer, so avoid this short stretch by continuing up the roadside for another hundred yards and leave on a wide cinder track to the left near the cattle gird. This is joined by the overgrown footpath in fifty yards or so; and gives a pleasant off-road saunter on the level, with excellent views into the valley below and across to Danby Rigg beyond.

Towards the end of the last glaciation large lakes were impounded in the Esk valley and its tributaries, as ice blocked their outlet. This left Castleton Rigg ahead of you and Danby Rigg across the valley as fingers of land projecting into the icy water.

In about 300 yards the track starts to descend towards the farm below; so keep your height by taking a clearly defined grassy track heading up at 45 degrees to the right. This leads you up to join the ridge road again near a walled paddock. Cross the unfenced road and pick up a track in the grass parallel to and some ten yards to the right (west) of the road before continuing your walk southwards. In good weather this is a joy to walk with fine views on both sides of the ridge which climbs gently towards the horizon.

Very soon, you'll spot on the road verge to your left a road junction sign. If you're opting for the shorter round, you need to walk across to the road and take this left fork (see box), rejoining the main route close to Ainthorpe at point C on the map (see below).

Confident walkers armed with refreshments and a good pair of legs can continue

From Castelton Rigg

on the track through the grass, enjoying the heather clad slopes. Be aware that the path in the grass eventually follows into a dead end in a former quarry close to the false summit on the horizon, and there is unfortunately no track following the crest of the ridge, although experienced strong walkers could follow the crest line across the open moor through the heather. Accordingly the easiest forward route (apart from walking along the road verge for a mile which is an option if you don't mind the passing traffic) is to slowly make your way downhill on the right towards the very quiet road accessing the isolated farms you can see below you to the west of the ridge.

When you reach this, follow this road, bearing to the left keeping on the tarmac as the road starts to re-ascend the Rigg near Brown Hill House. This steady climb, steep near the top, is accomplished without the intrusion of more than the very occasional vehicle, if that; and when you rejoin the main moor road, turn right, keeping on the verge and heading into what looks and feels like infinity, the level horizon which marks the high plateau of the North York Moors. It's now a much shorter walk along the verge, maybe some 400 yards, before you take the road running off on the left, a sharp turn

> ### 🚶 LESS WALKING, MORE BEER?
>
> The short cut shown on the map uses quiet lanes and a good bridleway to reduce the circuit length by 40% whilst still visiting briefly the summit ridge of Castleton Rigg: from point (**A** ⊕ 683066) look out for the road sign advertising a left turn and walk across to take this lane down off the Rigg. It descends pleasantly to Crag House Farm. From there walk east, passing the beautiful but isolated parish church of St Hilda's and its quiet churchyard, worth the small detour. Take the second left turn, Tofts Lane, at a staggered cross roads and look for one of the minimalist bridleway signs on the right after five minutes, heading through the fields towards the farm about 500 yards away. The bridleway passes through the farmyard at Rowantree Farm and takes you up to merge with another quiet lane at point (**C** ⊕ 705074) just south of Ainthorpe.

dropping steeply downhill into the valley below. There's no footway on this lane to Danby Botton but traffic is very light.

Pass a very basic Wesleyan chapel at the foot of the hill, keep straight ahead at the junction to arrive at a four way junction with Botton village centre (such as it is) signed to the right. Here, bear left, and walk along the lane for a few minutes, before taking the signed path up the farm track just beyond a little lay-by. Go through the farm yard and bear right onto a path heading south for a few yards before heading uphill again through the field and then up through rougher scrub, making for the top corner of the plantation of trees to the right of you. At this point (**B** 💮 700047) you'll find a gate onto the open moor.

Again, in summer the path is rather encroached by bracken, but it now zig zags, first to your left, towards a very impressive henge-like outcrop of gritstone, then back to the right, up the steepest part of the climb onto Danby Rigg above. The path should be quite visible at all seasons.

The gradient eases and you'll want to pause to gather your breath and admire the fine views. The path now curves back to the left again and leads you across the plateau of the Rigg, towards a helpful pair

The Fox & Hounds on the green at Ainthorpe

of cairns (piles of stones) some 300 yards distant. If you look to the far left on this stretch you should, in good visibility, be able to discern the distinctive summit of Roseberry Topping on the horizon. At over 1000' the unmistakeable cone shaped summit has been compared, probably favourably by Yorkshiremen, with the slightly higher Matterhorn! Beyond it, but well hidden, lies the industrial estuary of Teesside.

In summer the plateau of the Rigg is covered in purple swathes of heather and looks very attractive. Follow this north easterly trajectory for some ten minutes until, by a small pile of stones, you reach the edge of the plateau and the path ahead drops more steeply into Little Fryup Dale. Here, bear left on a path which keeps to the level. Pass a stone pillar and triangulation point after another ten minutes but keep ahead on the track. A little distance beyond the Trig point,

a wide bridleway comes up the escarpment from the right and joins your path. Bear left merging onto this wider path, and from here on in, it's a pleasant and easy walk across the rest of the Rigg gently downhill towards Ainthorpe. It's a good mile but if time is moving on you can maintain quite a good pace down this well-defined track, until you reach the motor road. Bear left and within fifty yards you'll spot the farm track on the left signed to Rowantree Farm at (**C** ⊕ 705074). This is the point at which the short cut route rejoins the 'yellow brick road'.

It's a few minutes further down the road into Ainthorpe, with its village green. The pretty, loose-knit village is typical of the area, with sandstone buildings offset by red pantiles. Overlooking the green in an eviable location is the Fox & Hounds, which given the long distance you've already walked may appeal for a restorative; but they do need to

Descent into Danby Dale

Downe Arms, Castleton

up their game as regards beer quality, which is why it doesn't make an entry here. It's about two thirds of a mile to the next pub, along the road but with the benefit of a footpath most of the way; continue down the street beyond the pub, bearing right at the junction and then on to Danby, passing over the railway line and station. As you begin to climb the hill the **Duke of Wellington** lies on the right, beyond the little village green. This 18th century pub-cum-hotel is a large stone building on a corner site, with a friendly licensee who keeps an interesting range of locally-brewed, well-kept ales: Daleside Bitter, one from Copper Dragon, and a rotating guest. There is no lunchtime food for non residents, but very close by, behind the pub to the right I warmly recommend the excellent Stonehouse bakers which provides sandwiches, pastries and other treats, whilst the Moors Visitor Centre is also nearby.

Opposite the Duke, take the lane signed for Castleton. Once again there's little realistic alternative but to walk along the roadside to reach Castleton, although fortunately the road isn't too busy. Cross the River Esk before the road eventually starts to climb up to the village. Once Castleton was the principal town serving Upper Eskdale; it had a weekly market and annual cheese, wool and cattle

fairs. These days it's rather sleepier, apart from traffic zooming down the hill, so watch out as you ascend into the village centre where you'll find the **2 Downe Arms**. Housed in an attractive gritstone building it is a regular entry, like the other pubs in this walk, in the *Good Beer Guide*. Black Sheep Best Bitter and Camerons Strongarm are the regulars, along with up to two changing guests. There's an extensive food menu.

The comfortable, carpeted bar has a real fire but if the weather's in your favour there is seating outside at both the front and the rear, where a patio garden looks out south with fine views south towards the Moors.

If you're relying on the train you need to look at your timetable before setting out from the Downe Arms. It's less than a mile to the station but there is the Eskdale Inn to consider. Once more a stretch of road walking beckons: take the road opposite the Downe Arms leading towards the station. It takes you back downhill and you rejoin the outward route close to the river bridge. Just beyond, and only a couple of minutes from the station, the **3 Eskdale Inn** has benefited from a decent makeover in both the décor and the beer range. Service is friendly in the two interconnected rooms. North Yorkshire's Eskd'ale and another guest in summer complement the Black Sheep and Tetley Bitters; and Black Dragon cider is a regular too. Good value food is available throughout the day. If you miss the train I recommend another beer…

Grosmont & the North York Moors Railway

Railway lovers will place this great circuit at the top of their list as it offers not only the prospect of a trip on one of Britain's best steam heritage lines, but also a visit to Grosmont, which is itself almost a preserved railway village, clustered around the North York Moors Railway's busy headquarters. Railway history abounds as the walk visits George Stephenson's old (1836) incline, the forerunner of the more modern railway up to Goathland; and the super Birch Hall Inn, the most unspoilt pub in the Moors National Park. The stiff climb *en route* to Egton is rewarded not just by great views of the rural valley of the Murk Esk River but also by the idyllically sited Horseshoe Hotel, but can be avoided by the faint-hearted or even visited by rail from Grosmont later in the day. Navigation is generally straightforward and should present few problems.

- **Start/finish:** Grosmont, railway station (National Rail; and North York Moors Railway, NYMR)

- **Access:** Good rail service from Whitby (5 miles) & Middlesbrough, or Pickering via NYMR

- **Distance:** 7 miles (11.3 km)

- **OS map:** Explorer OL27

- **Key attractions:** North York Moors steam railway and engine sheds; Goathland ('Heartbeat country'; 1 mile); Birch Hall Inn, historic pub; Whitby (5 miles)

- **THE PUBS:** Birch Hall Inn, Beck Hole; Horseshoe Hotel, Egton Bridge; Station Tavern, Grosmont. Try also: Postgate Inn, Egton Bridge

- **Timing tips:** The Birch Hall Inn opens at 11am daily, and is best enjoyed early before the tiny bars fill up with visitors in the season. Note also that the lunchtime food service at the Horseshoe ends at 2pm. The early (8.50am) train from Whitby is recommended.

Beck Hole hamlet nestles in the Murk Esk valley

Start from the centre of Grosmont by the level crossing. The whole village is almost as if in a timewarp, especially here where there always seems to be activity centred on the railway, with its lovingly restored station decked out in the post-1947 livery of the North Eastern Region of British Rail. Just on the east side of the crossing and almost opposite the Station Inn, take the footpath signed to the engine sheds, passing some pretty cottages before crossing the river on a dinky little metal suspension bridge alongside the line. Fork left by the church immediately (unless you wish to visit the railway sheds first) and walk up through the trees (signed 'Goathland Rail Trail'). At the waymark through the gate, leave the rail trail already and instead turn left down the hill ('Murk Esk'). Bear right in another 100 yards (still signed 'Murk Esk'), down steps and crossing the river atmospherically on a narrow footbridge. Now, reach a narrow and quiet lane and bear right ('Doctor's Wood').

The next couple of miles involve a steady climb up through the wooded valley side and out onto the moorland above. Continue on the tarred lane (disregard a second sign for Doctor's Wood), which climbs, steeply for a bit, onto a bank high above the river

valley over to your right. In about five minutes, just before reaching a metal gate, divert onto a path heading right into the trees. This pleasant and well-worn path winds more gently (but still uphill) through the woods, and you may be able to hear (and, in winter at least, see) the work going on in the railway sheds far below. The path levels off and becomes an easy stroll. Join a path merging from the left, whereafter you should be able to pick out an intermittent line of flagstones in the vegetation, suggesting that this might have been quite an ancient trackway.

After a few more minutes' walk, cross a wooden stile and emerge into the bottom of a field, returning to the woodland via a stile at the far end, but then almost immediately left again into another field, with the best view yet of the wooded Murk Esk Valley. If you're very lucky and a train is passing, you might catch a glimpse of steam wafting up out of the trees below.

KEY

🚶 Walk start/finish

▬ ▬ ▬ ▬ Walk route

•••••• Alternative route

Early morning steam at Grosmont

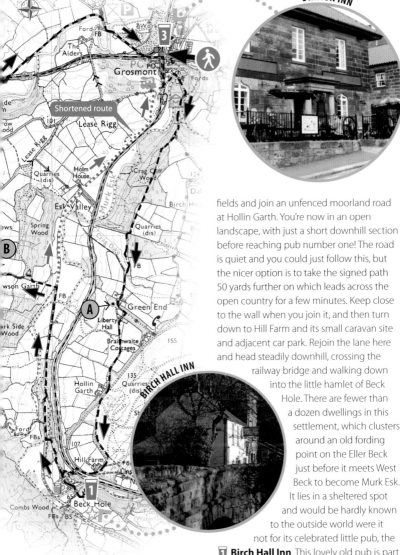

STATION INN

BIRCH HALL INN

fields and join an unfenced moorland road at Hollin Garth. You're now in an open landscape, with just a short downhill section before reaching pub number one! The road is quiet and you could just follow this, but the nicer option is to take the signed path 50 yards further on which leads across the open country for a few minutes. Keep close to the wall when you join it, and then turn down to Hill Farm and its small caravan site and adjacent car park. Rejoin the lane here and head steadily downhill, crossing the railway bridge and walking down into the little hamlet of Beck Hole. There are fewer than a dozen dwellings in this settlement, which clusters around an old fording point on the Eller Beck just before it meets West Beck to become Murk Esk. It lies in a sheltered spot and would be hardly known to the outside world were it not for its celebrated little pub, the

1 Birch Hall Inn. This lovely old pub is part of a terrace, and has two small bar rooms (the 'big' and the 'small') separated by a sweet shop. Nothing much has changed here for years, not even the licensee, though there's now a very nice little garden area by the river. Simple food offerings like pies and rolls complement the excellent beer on three handpumps. The house beer, Beckwater, is brewed by the North Yorkshire brewery.

Emerge after a few more minutes onto a bridleway ('Goathland') and walk up to the farmstead at Green End (**A** 825035). Here the path takes a 50-yard detour to the left, on the tarred lane, bearing right around the house on a waymarked route, on the contour once again, on a track, which at first might be muddy in the vicinity of the farm buildings. Now you pass through several

Stepping stones at Egton Bridge

If you have other books from the CAMRA Pub Walks series, you'll know that I not infrequently sound off about abysmal pub signs. I'm happy to say that the excellent sign on the wall of the Birch Hall Inn showing the local gorge was painted by Royal Academy artist Algernon Newton (1880–1968), who lived in Beck Hole during the war years and gave the painting to the landlady in gratitude for happy hours spent. It has faded a bit as it has hung there since 1944!

For those interested in TV soaps, Goathland, the village a mile further up the railway line, was the setting for *Heartbeat*. It also has a station, so if you spend too long in the Birch Hall Inn, the quickest way back to Grosmont is to head down to the incline track via the path almost opposite the pub and turn left for the NYMR station!

If you're continuing to the Horseshoe Inn, remember that food service stops at 2pm and you should allow 90 minutes for a leisurely walk to reach it. The route continues by retracing your steps back across the bridge and to the far end of the hamlet, by the foot of the steep hill out, and take the signed footpath ('Egton & Egton Bridge') on the left, a pretty path into the woodland. At a path junction, bear left via a duckboard to join the old railway incline, now the Rail Trail

path (see box). Bear right. You can see the remains of the old rail bridge over the Murk Esk in a few minutes as you follow the wide and well-used footpath through trees and across a meadow. The track re-crosses the river; a hundred yards beyond, look out for a (slightly obscure) stile on the left giving access to a track of sorts heading straight up the hillside. Here, you can return easily to Grosmont by continuing along the trail (see alternative route on map), but for the hardy, surmount the stile and head up the hill. The climb here is the steepest of the day by some distance, so taking your time is recommended. You may be rewarded, as I was, with the sight and sound of a steam train in the valley below as you toil uphill.

The path you've been following becomes more obscure the higher you climb, but simply keep close to the right-hand boundary of the field, well away from the line of telegraph posts heading uphill, and you will emerge through a metal gate just to the right of the farm buildings above you, onto a farm track at (**B** 🕑 815037). Have a rest here! Ignore the waymark ahead by the stables, but instead turn right through another metal gate, and look for a five-bar wooden gate 20 yards beyond on the left. When you're at the gate, you'll see a waymark. Pass through the gate and head up into field beyond – uphill again – keeping close to the wire fence on the left. If you pause and look behind you on this stretch, you should be able to see a gigantic pyramid on the horizon. This is the RAF Fylingdales early warning station. It's a relief when the gradient finally levels off as you approach High Burrows Farm, joining the little lane to the left of the buildings via a couple of step stiles. A good place to pause and enjoy that little snack you put in your rucksack this morning… the good news is that at about 160 metres (500 feet) this is the highest point of the day and that it's downhill now all the way to the next pub!

The signed footpath continues straight across. Keep right and over the stile almost at the foot, bearing slightly left towards the telegraph pole and yellow post, where you'll pass through a gap and down to the gate and yellow marker below you in the next field. Now simply follow straight ahead, keeping to the right-hand edge of the long, narrow field with a line of telegraph posts on the left, and a house ahead to your right. This is Low Hollins Farm. Exit the field at the end of the wall of the building via a five-bar wooden gate and join the motor road down the grassy (and later stony) farm track. Bear right. A short stretch

Woodland path ascending from Grosmont

of road walking ensues, but clearly signed just beyond Blue Beck Cottage is a path on the right. It's a pleasant walk down through the woodland with views through the trees of Egton Manor; but it's steep in paces and in muddy conditions may be slippery, so take care. Emerge on the road at Egton Bridge, and turn left here for the very short walk down to the **2 Horseshoe Hotel**. Set back from the road in an idyllic location, with a grassy garden in front and the river immediately behind, this family-run hotel is a superb spot for a well-earned lunch washed down with a pint. The small but atmospheric public bar (the far door, beyond the hotel entrance) is welcoming if the weather doesn't allow you to sit outside. There are two handpumps dispensing a changing variety of (often local) beers at the time of writing, so you may well strike it lucky. Food is excellent if my experience is anything to go by.

The Birch Hall Inn, with its two bars and shop

Postgate Inn, Egton Bridge

Leaving the Horseshoe, the signed path ('stepping stones') leaves from the hotel driveway (retrace your inward steps for 20 yards). It's an interesting path over the bifurcated river hidden in the trees. Two sets of high stepping stones should be able to cope with most water levels. Cross a mill race and pass the old mill to join a road, turning right to walk down and reach a T-junction. (If you don't fancy the stepping stones, then, to reach the same point, simply return to the road and bear left.) If you want to call in at the **4 Postgate Inn** and/or catch the train, the station (and inn) lie a short distance up the road to the left. The Postgate Inn – formerly the Station Inn but renamed in honour of Fr Oliver Postgate, a Catholic Martyr who was hanged at York – is a handsome stone building and serves a couple of real ales, at present Adnams Broadside and Black Sheep Bitter. It's open all day in the summer, but closes from 2.30 to 6.30 in winter.

Before this, just before you reach the church, the onward walking route to Grosmont is signed off to the right. This is the old Barnards Toll Road, passing through the parkland of the Egton Estate, a permissive path rather than a right of way. Halfway along, the old toll house displays an old table of charges. It's about a mile and a half of easy and, in the right conditions, pleasant walking before you join the motor road just outside Grosmont. Turn right here, and cross the river before walking into the village. If you're by any chance doing the walk later in the day, the **5 Crossing Club** with its CAMRA awards and impressive selection of real ales is open to card-carrying CAMRA members from 8pm. Otherwise for a well-earned final drink it's the **3 Station Tavern**. It's an imposing and well-proportioned stone building with fancy windows and a classical portico dating from 1836; you'll find it just over the level crossing, and in good weather you can sit on the front patio and watch activity on the line. Expect up to three beers, with Camerons Strongarm and Black Sheep Best Bitter the regulars.

PUB INFORMATION

1 BIRCH HALL INN
Beck Hole, YO22 5LE
01947 896245 • www.beckhole.info
Opening hours: 11-11

2 HORSESHOE HOTEL
Egton Bridge, YO21 1XE •
01947 895245 • www.egtonbridgehotel.co.uk
Opening hours: 11.30-11

3 STATION TAVERN
Grosmont, YO22 5PA •
01947 895060 • www.stationtavern-grosmont.co.uk
Opening hours: 12-11 summer; 12-3, 5.30-11 winter

Try also:

4 POSTGATE INN
Egton Bridge, YO21 1UX •
01947 895241 • www.postgateinn.com
Opening hours: 11-11 summer; 11-2.30, 6.30-11 winter

5 CROSSING CLUB
Co-operative Building, Front Street, Grosmont, YO22 5QE
07766 197744 • twitter.com/Grosmont
Opening hours: 8pm-11

Whitby's historic hinterland

The attractive countryside inland from Whitby is often overlooked as most visitors who venture out of town make for the admittedly excellent coast path. This short little circuit (with the option of making it shorter still) allows plenty of time for the walking imbiber to explore historic Whitby itself (not to mention its improving pub scene), and offers plenty of interest whether or not you know the town already. It includes plenty of history, not least the mightily impressive Larpool Viaduct, now open to walkers and cyclists as part of Sustrans' National Cycle Network North Sea Coast route. In wet weather parts of the walk, especially the flags on the Monk's Path, can be slippery.

▶ **Start/finish:** Whitby rail station

▶ **Access:** By bus and rail from Leeds and York

▶ **Distance:** 6.4 miles (10.3 km) excluding Whitby pubs

▶ **OS map:** Explorer OL27

▶ **Key attractions:** Whitby Abbey ruins and other attractions; Larpool Viaduct; Monk's Path; Beacon Farm tea rooms, Sneaton (beacon-farmicecream.co.uk); Robin Hood's Bay (8 miles)

▶ **THE PUBS:** Wilson Arms, Sneaton; Bridge Inn, Ruswarp; Black Horse, Little Angel, Station Inn, all Whitby

▶ **Timing tips:** The Wilson Arms is open at lunchtimes only on a Sunday, but if you have the stamina the full round is still a worthwhile walk. If not, take the shorter option and head for the Bridge Inn, which serves food each day except Monday.

Whitby's coastal charm can overshadow its other attractions

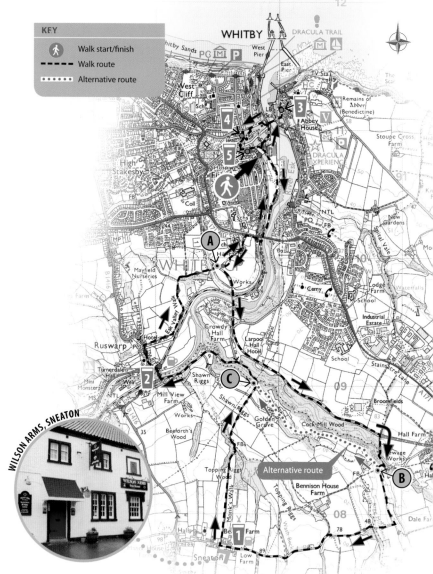

KEY

🚶 Walk start/finish

- - - - Walk route

••••• Alternative route

WILSON ARMS, SNEATON

Alternative route

🚶 Starting at Whitby rail station – one of the few in the country shared between National Rail services and a preserved line, the popular North York Moors Railway (see Walk 9) – turn right and walk up past the Tourist Information Centre and the Co-op supermarket, along the river estuary towards the marina. At the far end of the car park, look for a signed footpath

leading alongside the railway line to Ruswarp (pronounced 'Russup'), beside a pedestrian level crossing. Ignore the former and, instead, carefully cross the railway before heading left along the track to join a road by a terrace of new houses. As the road curves away to the right, head up the steep asphalt footpath ahead. This path offers good views over Whitby harbour as you ascend, before reaching the busy A171 Scarborough Road. Cross carefully, bear right and follow the path running parallel to the road on the wooded margin, before turning left at Caedmon School. Walking up the school drive, keeping the school on your right, head towards the school playing fields; then turn sharp right and follow the signed right of way across the fields for some 400 yards before the signed path leads out and onto the old Whitby–Scarborough railway line, the 'cinder track' ahead (**A** 🗺️ 896099).

Pretty cottages at Ruswarp

Turn left and head towards the Larpool Viaduct. This striking brick-built viaduct was completed in 1884 and its 13 arches span the Esk at a height of 120 feet. Of course, you get a better view from a distance rather than walking across it! The line was closed in March 1965 as part of the 'Beeching Axe' but is now part of the North Sea Coast walking and cycle route.

Carry on down the old track with the imposing old Larpool Hall Hotel above you, away to your left. Now you have about a mile of easy walking along the old trackbed (heavily recolonised by nature) before you come to a small stone bridge with steps on the left leading down to a footpath fingerpost. Follow this to pass under the old line, then head steeply downhill through the pretty Cock Mill Wood on an old packhorse path, which has rather disintegrated and can be very slippery in the wet, but has sections of old flagstones – one of the old 'trods' that were once very common in this part of Yorkshire (see box). Cross a footbridge over Stainsacre Beck, then up the other side for 100 yards or so and bear right; this brings you up to join a wide track by a gate labelled 'Watson's Farm' (**B** 🗺️ 908084).

This is the point at which a decision must be made: the 'long round', or the 'short round'? As indicated above, the Wilson Arms is closed at lunchtimes except on Sunday, but the longer walk passing that pub, even if closed, is still recommended if you have

the energy and stamina to keep going until you eventually arrive at Ruswarp. And, as an alternative, in Sneaton you'll find Beacon Farm, where you can get ice cream and teas!

If you're doing the short-cut, turn right on the track by the gate and follow this through the pretty woodland. It soon turns into a metalled road, and after a mile or so you'll reach the tiny hamlet of Golden Grove and the striking Cock Mill Hall. The road heads left over a bridge, but at this point fork right (or straight on) past some renovated stables and, by a house ahead, left down a stone track into the woods, passing the well-sited Waterfall Cottage overlooking the falls on Rigg Mill Beck. You'll soon arrive at a point where the 'long round' rejoins from the left over a footbridge (**C** 🗺️ 898091).

If you opt for the 'long round', turn left and follow the good track – which becomes grassy after about five minutes – through a metal gate in another four or five minutes, then turn into the grassy opening on the right and head through the six-bar red metal gate into a very steep and narrow sunken trackway. In summer it is almost closed over, as a tunnel, with vegetation. Take care down here as, again, it can be slippery. At the foot, cross the little stream and continue ahead up the far side, still in woodland, reaching the road to Bennison House Farm. Turn left here, and simply follow the very quiet lane, which soon leads into Sneaton village.

THE TRODDS OF NORTH-EAST YORKSHIRE

'Trod' is an old word for a path, but in its revived usage the essential feature of a trod is the single row of large stone flags. There is no particular reason why trods were constructed and, although they are even sometimes referred to as 'monks' trods', they are by no means associated exclusively with monastic properties, though it is probable that monastic labour helped to create them. Most of them were simply early forms of roadway such as the packhorse trails of Calderdale in West Yorkshire. They are in evidence on much of this walk but particularly on the stretch north from Sneaton, shown on the maps as the 'Monk's Path'; and again on leaving Ruswarp heading across the marsh towards the old railway track.

You can't miss the 🚩 **Wilson Arms** on the main street, a handsome listed 18th-century building. As already mentioned, getting inside can prove difficult; but if you do, it makes a good refuelling stop in just the right spot and, in winter, a chance to warm up in front of an open fire. Beer-wise, Black Sheep Bitter plus a changing guest are the current offerings, and on Sundays lunch is also served. If it's closed, the Beacon Farm ice cream parlour and tea rooms will loom all the more attractively; they are just a little further on, on the right. Even this will be shut on Monday and Tuesday during winter, though…

The onward route continues down the village street for a short while: look for the bridleway sign on the opposite side of the road, but nonetheless pointing to the right. Head down this straight track leading north and gently downhill on the so-called Monk's Path. It gets steeper and more atmospheric as you near the stream and descend on a flagged track – it takes little imagination to transport yourself back to the days of monks heading to Whitby Abbey. Cross the stream and head up the grassy lane to join the minor road. Here, head straight across (no sign) and start a second descent into Cock Mill Wood. It's every bit as steep as the earlier episode. The well-built path leads down to a pair of footbridges at point (**C** 🕓 898091).

Now it's a pretty simple stroll down the pleasant wooded valley accompanied by the Stainsacre Beck, until you meet another road on a sharp bend. There's now a stretch of road walking: follow the road downhill, but take the usual care when there is no footway. The road bears left when it reaches the Esk Valley and leads into Ruswarp and its distinctive girder bridge over the river. Cross this and the level crossing by the station to the 🚩 **Bridge Inn**. Open all day from noon (except winter Mondays), the Bridge Inn is a pleasant two-room pub (with a rear games room in addition) and offers three cask beers, Theakston Bitter and up to two guests, which could come from far or near (Adnams Bitter was on when I visited). As stated earlier, food is available except on Mondays, and on Sunday there's a carvery.

Right opposite the pub is the station for Whitby (four trains daily; note that NYMR trains don't stop here), and also a permissive path back to Whitby which is the quickest route, not much over a mile, following the railway. It does offer super views of Larpool Viaduct, but I would recommend the alternative route described here for greater interest and not much greater distance. Head left up the hill in the main street of Ruswarp passing the church. There are some pretty cottages to admire, but the traffic is somewhat oppressive. (Ruswarp was also

Whale jawbone arch, Whitby

track, through the trees, and then you come upon a deep cutting, once occupied by the old railway track from Whitby which curved and climbed sharply to meet the line from Scarborough. (You can see the pair of old tracks clearly on the Ordnance Survey map; and – a real treat for railway buffs – you can watch a train undertake this manoeuvre and cross the viaduct in a piece of 1960s archive film on the Yorkshire Film Archive's website www.yorkshirefilmarchive.com)

Descend into the cutting and mount the other side, just as steep, followed by a short walk across to the cinder track that you met on the outward leg. Now, simply retrace your steps across the school playing fields, down to the road, and cross as per the outward leg and down into Whitby, making once more for the railway station and tourist office.

Once in Whitby there are plenty of pubs to choose from. I recommend you start by following the river to the right and crossing the swing bridge. Whitby wears its hordes of tourists pretty well, particularly on the east bank of the river, where narrow lanes and old buildings enable it to retain some of its salty atmosphere. The best of the streets are Sandgate and the section of Church Street parallel to it, north of the bridge and on the approach to the Abbey steps.

It's down here close to the market hall that you'll find Whitby's most unspoilt pub, the **3 Black Horse**. With a splendid multi-roomed interior, this harbourside gem has changed little since it was built some

the name of a celebrated dog that played a significant part in the fight to save the Settle–Carlisle Railway in the 1980s. To find out more, look him up on your favourite search engine!)

Just before the Jacobean Ruswarp Hall Hotel on the right, a path ('Whitby 1 mile') heads right alongside a wall and passes some cottages. It leads out onto a low-lying meadow with the railway on your right and a tall grassy cliff away to your left. Follow the path along a well-engineered causeway of neat flags with the top of the brick viaduct in view across to the right, before ascending the wooded hillside on a flight of steep steps to a fingerboard. Take the right-hand option, signed to the marina and cinder

The imposing ruins of Whitby Abbey

130 years ago. The front room with fitted benches and an ancient bar counter is one to enjoy at quieter times; the rear bar and snug is mainly long and narrow. Five cask ales are served, with Adnams Southwold Bitter and local brewery Black Dog's Rhatas the anchor beers, supported by three changing guests. Food is mainly of the tapas variety, but if you want to eat in the town, fish and chips is still Whitby's staple diet. Either way, this is a great pub for whiling away an hour rewarding yourself for putting a few miles behind you, and the timeless interior would be complete with a fixture of ancient Oates & Green Halifax porcelain in the gents… but alas! You'll have to look into the Elsinore on Flowergate across the river to get that real deal in Whitby!

Back across the bridge, head up the narrow passage directly ahead by the Golden Lion. This opens into Flowergate, by the art gallery dedicated to the work of celebrated local Victorian photographer Frank Meadow Sutcliffe. Walk up Flowergate until you reach the **4** **Little Angel** on the corner of Brunswick Street. This much-altered multi-room pub has perhaps the most interesting range of beers in town at the moment and won the 2015 local CAMRA award. Six changing beers are available, and you may be as lucky as I was on my last visit when one of them was the award-winning Elland 1872 Porter in superb condition. My one gripe here is the presence in every corner of a widescreen TV, so I was also unable to escape being force-fed the Champions League football. If the management is reading: please, we don't *all* want this while we're out drinking!

Station Inn, Whitby

To round off the day, walk down Brunswick Street to the bottom of the road and bear left back towards the rail and bus stations. Right opposite, and therefore perfectly placed if you're heading out by public transport, stands the **5** **Station Inn**. The exterior is a lop-sided oddity in a rather failed inter-war mock Tudor pastiche, but this is soon forgiven once inside, for again the multi-roomed interior has survived, with a front snug, a large rear public bar and a side lounge. Eight beers, including house beer Platform 3 from Whitby brewery and four others on rotation, offer a plentiful choice in what has been rightly called the discerning traveller's waiting room.

PUB INFORMATION

1 **WILSON ARMS**
Beacon Way, Sneaton, YO22 5HS •
01947 602552 • www.thewilsonarms-whitby.co.uk
Opening hours: 6.30-11; 12-4, 6.30-11 Sun; closed Mon winter

2 **BRIDGE INN**
High Street, Ruswarp, YO21 1NJ
01947 602780
Opening hours: 12-11; 4-11 Mon in winter

3 **BLACK HORSE**
91 Church Street, Whitby, YO22 4BH
01947 602906 • www.the-black-horse.com
Opening hours: 11-11; 12-10.30 Sun

4 **LITTLE ANGEL**
18 Flowergate, Whitby, YO21 3BA
01947 820475 • www.littleangelwhitby.co.uk
Opening hours: 11.30-11; 11-11 Sun

5 **STATION INN**
New Quay Road, Whitby, YO21 1DH
01947 603937 • www.stationinnwhitby.co.uk
Opening hours: 10-midnight; 10-11.30 Sun

Black Horse, Whitby

West Yorkshire

→

Three cloughs & a canal: from Hebden Bridge

The accurately self-styled 'Pennine centre' – having seen its fortunes change from prosperous mill town to hippy hangout – is now going upmarket again, reflected in some smart new shops. But one thing that remains constant is the wonderful scenery, with several deeply wooded valleys (or cloughs in local parlance) converging on the ancient packhorse bridge over Hebden Water that gave the town its name. Its predecessor from domestic weaving days, Heptonstall, sits atop the hill above its younger progeny.

> **Start/finish:**
> Hebden Bridge town centre

> **Access:** Good rail links from Leeds/Bradford and Manchester

> **Distance:** 7.2 miles (11.6 km)

> **OS map:** Explorer OL21

> **Key attractions:**
> Industrial history (see www.powerinthelandscape.co.uk); Heptonstall, old weaving village; Rochdale Canal; superb walking country

> **THE PUBS:** White Lion, Heptonstall; New Delight Inn, Stubbing Wharf, Fox & Goose, Calan's Micropub, all Hebden Bridge. Try also: Old Gate Bar & Restaurant, Hebden Bridge

> **Timing tips:** Calan's in Hebden Bridge is closed on Monday and Tuesday; the White Lion (an hour or so into the walk) opens at mid-day so, unless extending the first leg of the walk, don't set off too early! Note also the afternoon closure (and Monday limited opening) at the New Delight.

The eponymous packhorse bridge in Hebden Bridge

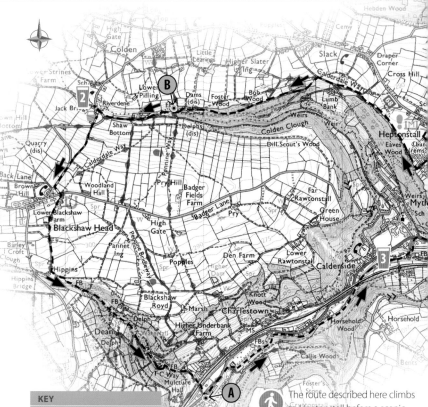

KEY

🚶 Walk start/finish

- - - - - Walk route

A hillside path in Hebden Bridge

🚶 The route described here climbs to Heptonstall before a scenic high-level walk to the head of Colden Clough and the uniquely named New Delight Inn, returning to the Rochdale Canal via picturesque Jumble Hole Clough with its ruined mill. Pubs are well spaced out, and the general pub scene hereabouts has improved immeasurably, underscored by two welcome new developments, namely the community buy-out of the Fox & Goose and very recently the opening of a new micropub in town.

It's very easy to locate the quaint old packhorse bridge in the centre of town: it's on Bridge Gate, 50 yards upstream from the main road bridge over Hebden Water. The first part of this route follows part of a waymarked trail to Hardcastle Crags, a popular local beauty spot (if you wish, you can pick up the accompanying leaflet, 'Three Waymarked Walks', in the local Tourist Office). Walk further up pedestrianised Bridge Gate to St Georges Square and cross this bridge (between the Shoulder

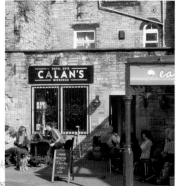

Calan's Micropub in Hebden Bridge   **Fox & Goose**

of Mutton and Bridge Mill) to turn immediately right onto a riverside walkway. This turns into a service road and leads to Victoria Road. You'll re-cross Hebden Water and swing left onto a terraced street. Third right is Windsor Road – turn up here as far as the next turning left. Follow this street down to the quaint Foster Mill packhorse bridge at the end. As soon as you cross this you're out of town. Leave the waymarked trail here and carry on uphill on the good path lined with stone setts, climbing steeply onto the hillside.

Bear right halfway up, at the first opportunity, onto a level, walled path, passing some attractive old stone houses, which almost seem to grow out of the vegetation, and enjoying fine views over the wooded valley of Hebden Water below. Cross a wider roadway, which runs downhill, and a few yards further along, at a fork of paths, follow the Calderdale Way link path (straight ahead, on the level); but, in another 100 yards, fork left at the next division of paths to continue, uphill again now, through pleasant woodland. Emerge onto a quiet tarred lane and turn right to head downhill now for a short distance towards a stone house. Just beyond, the lanes fork: bear left (at the Hebden Hay Scout Hostel sign), and immediately you'll notice an unsigned earthen track running quite steeply uphill into

the woods. Take this handy shortcut as far as yet another scissor junction of paths, and here, with the road wall in sight above you, turn sharply left back on yourself to join the road itself by a footpath sign ('public bridleway, Midgehole'; (**A** ⊕ 989286).

Cross the road and immediately opposite continue in the same direction, at a more gentle angle now, towards Heptonstall. This path was once part of an old packhorse route leading across the moors to Haworth. There are great views now across the valley to Chiserley and down into Hebden Bridge, before you emerge onto Northgate, now a quiet residential lane that leads down into Heptonstall village (see box) by the Cross Inn.

A few yards up the street on the right, the **White Lion**, once a rather austere hostelry, has been transformed by new licensees into a welcoming free house; the interior has been opened out but retains distinct areas with five cask ales (Thwaites Wainwright plus four changing guests, mainly from Yorkshire breweries) and traditional ciders, supplemented by an excellent food menu including a great range of vegetarian dishes. In winter there's a real fire to the room on the left; in summer you could try the little rear courtyard garden, which has been much improved.

Walk a little further up the Main Street on departure, bearing left on Church Street by the two churches (the ruined old one and the imposing newer one), then keeping the churchyard wall on your left as you swing round left again to rejoin the Calderdale Way (CW) at West Laithe (bear right), crossing a road and then bearing right (CW sign for Colden) on a walled path through a newish little housing estate to bring you very soon to the edge of a near precipice at the top edge of the wide, wooded valley of Colden Clough.

Turn right here and make your way carefully along the well-defined, but nonetheless rather uneven, path threading its way through some large sandstone outcrops. Take care on this 500-yard stretch before you emerge onto a tarred lane (signposted 'Lumb Mills'), where you head down the slope before bearing off to the right in another 100 yards (CW sign). Of interest here is that continuing down the tarred lane instead at this point would bring you to Lumb Bank, once the home of poet Ted Hughes, who captured this landscape so evocatively in his collection *Remains of Elmet*.

On the path disregard paths right and left and continue on the level, traversing a section of flagstones towards a house ahead. Beyond this, obeying the red waymarks of the Hebden Bridge Loop of the Pennine Way, follow the bridleway to the left, forking right after a further 100 yards, again obeying the waymarks. Note distant views now behind you back to the distinctive outline of Heptonstall church. The well-signed route, much lined with stone setts, now inexorably leads slowly down towards the wooded bottom of Colden Clough, which you eventually reach at a very pretty little clapper footbridge ((**B**) 968282). The little stream was once the power source for a

Ruins of the old church, Heptonstall

remarkable cascade of mills along the valley. You can read about these on the 'Power in the Landscape' website (www.powerinthe-landscape.co.uk). Cross here, and continue upstream on the south bank keeping close to the stream, joining a rough lane and emerging onto the motor road at the apex of a sharp bend. Now in sight, just beyond the campsite, is a well-earned second stop, the **2** **New Delight Inn**. Like the White Lion, this place has been reinvigorated under new management and is now able to make the most of its outstanding location. Inside there remain several interconnected rooms around the servery, with the room on the left retaining its flag flooring. It's a key outlet for the local Bridestones brewery: expect at least two of their beers on tap; with a couple of guests too, mainly from regional micros. Decent food is available – I would recommend the baguettes.

The homeward leg of the walk starts with retracing your steps up the short hill and

View down Colden Clough after leaving Heptonstall

continuing around the bend alongside the campsite (take care: no footpath) until you reach the bus stop, opposite the quaintly named terrace 'High Street' (!). Here, take the bridleway, which climbs steeply and soon merges with another road. Again follow the verge and walk into the hamlet of Black-shaw Head, passing the entry sign but then bearing left at another bus stop 40 yards beyond it. This lane soon reaches another road: cross straight over (CW sign) and bear right passing some attractive old stone buildings at Lower Blackshaw Farm Cottage; swing round this and look for another CW sign leading down a flagged path, passing a solitary wind turbine. Note Stoodley Pike in the distance. Be guided by the waymarks, which carry you around the next set of farm buildings and over several stiles, some requiring a degree of agility to negotiate! The going is gentle, downhill into the wooded Jumble Hole Clough. At a wooded spot by a very attractive mullioned house (Hippins) locate the CW Link path (signed), which leads off to the left here (don't continue along the frontage of the house). You come out briefly onto an open meadow, but just 40 yards on by the weathered old wooden signpost head left towards Jumble Hole Clough, the obvious

wooded valley on your right. It's fairly plain sailing now across a stile and down to cross a little beck and into the clough itself.

It's a delightful walk through this steep little valley and a treat to come upon the attractive ruins of Staups Mill, which dates from the late 18th century and in Victorian times was spin-ning cotton using water power from dams above it. Apart from a short climb beyond the mill, it's downhill all the way on the most obvious path, but, after meeting a wider, con-creted, vehicle track halfway down, cross the river on the bridge 50 steep yards beyond and continue downhill (follow Pennine Bridleway sign) close to the far side of the stream, and this will lead you unerringly down to the main Calder Valley bottom at Charlestown, where you bear to your left. To save walking along the busy A646 road, there's a fenced verge margin taking you along to the pedestrian crossing which enables you to navigate over the river and join the Rochdale canal towpath.

Now you have a pleasant stroll, still heading east, along the waterside, for less than a mile, as far as the **3** **Stubbing Wharf**. With a rear entrance giving directly onto the towpath (and canalside seating as well), this solid and cosy Victorian pub arranged on two levels, is well sited and very popular. It offers all-day

HEPTONSTALL

Visiting Heptonstall for the first time is a striking experi-ence. Now an out-of-the-way backwater, it is an old settle-ment and was once an impor-tant centre of the handloom weaving industry. The long upper-floor windows on many of the cottages on the main street testify to this; they were to let maximum daylight onto the looms. From Heptonstall, a network of packhorse paths (you have just walked up one) enabled pieces of cloth to be taken away for trade. Many of them journeyed by canal from the valley below and ended up in Halifax's superb Piece Hall, a unique building that

underwent major restoration in 2015. Ironically, the canal – and later the railway – played a part in the decline of the vil-lage, since the new settlement of Hebden Bridge was more convenient for transport. But once mechanised looms arrived, the whole industry moved east onto the coal-fields and Bradford became the undisputed wool manu-facturing centre of the world. Heptonstall was also the site of a battle in 1643 during the early part of the English Civil War; and as an important cen-tre for nonconformism, the octagonal Methodist chapel, the oldest still in continued

Canal scene at Hebden Bridge

use, was founded following the visit of John Wesley in 1764. Sylvia Plath's grave is in the churchyard; she was mar-ried to local poet Ted Hughes.

Clapper bridge over Colden Clough

food service in addition to a better-than-ever beer range, which includes Timothy Taylor's Landlord, Black Sheep Bitter and Copper Dragon's Golden Pippin, as well as a couple of guests and a real cider.

Continue along the towpath as far as the end of Lock 11 and look for a stone step stile in the low wall by the first of the five gable ends of the houses on the canalside, and down short Eton Street. Bear left at the end by the river, looking for an iron footbridge accessed via a short riverside path. Cross this and follow a small beck up to the main road. Now it's a very short walk to the right along the A646 before you come upon the **4** **Fox & Goose**. WARNING: take great care crossing the road here by the awkward junction to get to it. West Yorkshire's first community-owned pub came about as a result of a spirited campaign by locals, lovers of the pub from further afield, and several co-operative and community organisations. The aim was to prevent the loss of this well-loved free house or its takeover by a chain, following the illness of the long-standing landlady. Enough money was raised to buy the freehold and the place reopened in 2014. It remains, as it always was, a small, cosy and quite distinctive little haven where good beer, conversation and a warm welcome are the order of the day. Seven handpumps dispense a changing variety of interesting beers, but there's an impressive list of bottled beers too. An early summer beer festival is held (see pub's website for details).

From the Fox & Goose it's but a short walk along the main road back into town (though you can rejoin the towpath by the Co-op if you prefer). On the road you'll see the substantial **6** **Old Gate Bar & Restaurant**, which I recommend if you can accommodate this smart and cheerful bar-cum-restaurant in your itinerary. With nine handpumps you'll get the widest choice of ales in town here, as well as real cider and some foreign bottled offerings. The Old Gate is evidence enough of the steady gentrification of Hebden Bridge, and just over the bridge and round into Bridge Gate where you started is yet more, in the shape of **5** **Calan's Micropub**. In a little courtyard, this new micropub squeezes five handpumps into its compact servery. You can expect some interesting beers on sale, check the Facebook page for the latest line-up, but don't get here too late – like many micropubs, it closes earlier than 'late'!

Buses leave from round the corner, and the rail station is a few minutes' walk away.

PUB INFORMATION

1 **WHITE LION**
58 Towngate, Heptonstall, HX6 7NB
01422 842027
Opening hours: 12-midnight

2 **NEW DELIGHT INN**
Jack Bridge, Blackshaw Head, Hebden Bridge, HX7
7HT 01422 844628 • www.newdelightinn.co.uk
Opening hours: 12-3 (not Mon), 5-11; 12-11 Fri &
Sat; 12-10 Sun

3 **STUBBING WHARF**
King Street, Hebden Bridge, HX7 6LU
01422 844107 • www.stubbingwharf.com
Opening hours: 12-midnight (11 Sun)

4 **FOX & GOOSE**
7 Heptonstall Road, Hebden Bridge, HX7 6AZ
01422 648052 • www.foxandgoose.org
Opening hours: 12-midnight (2am Fri & Sat)

5 **CALAN'S MICROPUB**
3 The Courtyard, Bridge Gate, Hebden Bridge, HX7 8EX
07739 565983
Opening hours: closed Mon & Tue; 12-9 Wed & Thu;
12-10 Fri & Sat; 12-8 Sun

Try also:

6 **OLD GATE BAR & RESTAURANT**
1-5 Old Gate, Hebden Bridge, HX7 8JP
01422 843993 · www.oldgatehebden.co.uk
Opening hours: 10-midnight; 10-11 Sun

Brontë country: Haworth & Ponden

Haworth's steep, cobbled Main Street, bypassed by most traffic, has kept a good deal of its old charm, while the modern workaday commercial centre of town has moved to the area by the rail station. Of course, many visitors come for the Brontë connections (and fit walkers can detour to take in Top Withins, the ruined farmhouse said to be the inspiration for Wuthering Heights); but with the town tucked in under the backbone of the Pennines, this is also great walking country, with extensive views.

▷ **Start/finish:** Main Street, Haworth

▷ **Access:** Rail to Keighley or Hebden Bridge, then bus; or Worth Valley Railway from Keighley

▷ **Distance:** 7 miles (11.3 km)

▷ **OS map:** Explorer OL21

▷ **Key attractions:** Haworth; Keighley & Worth Valley Railway (www. kwvr.co.uk); Brontë literary connections.

▷ **THE PUBS:** Old Silent, Stanbury; Grouse Inn, Harehill; Fleece Inn, Haworth Old Hall, both Haworth

▷ **Timing tips:** Haworth makes a good base from which to start this walk; if coming from Leeds or Bradford, an early start is recommended, although both rural pubs on the round are open all day.

Across the Worth Valley near Stanbury

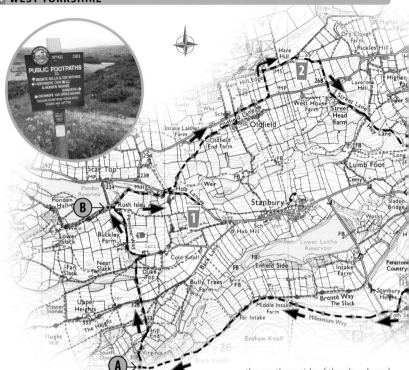

Pubs here are understandably food-oriented, but as with elsewhere in the region the beer range and quality has improved fast and all the entries here offer locally produced cask ales. The walk, though always on clear paths, takes one into the moors more so than most of the other walks in this collection; so caution in poor weather, particularly mist, is advised. Also, the first pub is a fair trek, so take refreshments.

The best way to arrive in Haworth is by the Keighley & Worth Valley Railway, one of the country's earliest preserved steam lines, which reopened in 1968 after closure by British Railways in 1962. From the station it's a short (signed) walk up through the park to the road junction by the Old Hall Inn at the foot of Main Street. Allowing time for sightseeing as required, head uphill to the signed footpath ('Penistone Hill') by the churchyard near the top of the hill on the left, before reaching the Black Bull. It leads along the southern side of the church and through the churchyard. Keep the gravestones on your right, leaving the churchyard via a kissing gate, walking past some allotments, and turn right at a path junction (signed 'Top Withins' and 'Brontë Falls'). Pass Balcony Farm. When you reach the road, cross straight over, pausing to take in the already extensive view behind you down the Worth Valley towards Keighley.

Now bear about 45 degrees left on the path ('Brontë Way') towards the summit of Penistone Hill, which is up on your left. After a further 200 yards, bear left again at the wooden signpost since this will take you to the actual summit, a little over 1000 feet in height and marked by a white triangulation pillar. You'll see it in a couple of minutes when you gain the brow of the ridge, almost under the line of telegraph wires. For relatively little effort the panorama is extensive and includes Ponden Reservoir, which you'll be visiting later in the walk.

Now continue by taking the track to the right of that by which you arrived, which

KEY

🚶 Walk start/finish

- - - - Walk route

Haworth's cobbled main street

In about 400 yards look out for some heathery spoil heaps on the left and, just by the path here, an interesting stone carving. Although there were several stone quarries hereabouts, this one was actually an old coalmine. It's capped and quite safe now. The carving shows the headstock above the mineshaft, connected to a horse-powered gin, which lowered men and equipment into the mine and lifted tubs of coal out. Interestingly, census records show that there were miners living in Haworth in 1841, but not in 1851, so probably the mining here ended during the 1840s.

will quickly take you back down to the wide sandy track of the main Brontë Way. Bear left on this, noting another, closer reservoir, Lower Laithe Reservoir – which came into view very shortly after leaving the summit point – and continue westwards on a wide and fairly level path, ignoring smaller offshoots.

Old Silent, Stanbury

The Brontë Bridge near Top Withins

and Brontë Falls (**A** 998358). It's a pretty, sheltered spot before you cross the stream and head up the steps to the kissing gate and sign-post. Here, sturdy souls armed with a map and refreshments can detour to Top Withins; it's about two miles there and back, so allow at least an hour. Lesser mortals take the right-hand path (Brontë Way) leading to another signpost. Turn right again and, at the following sign (you're heading diagonally right through a kissing gate), cross a ladder stile and the wide track and keep ahead, still on the Brontë Way ('Wycoller'). At yet another track (where returnees from Top Withins may rejoin), go straight across once again, now on the Pennine Way with its distinctive acorn symbol. The Pennine Way is well signed, so just look out for the waymarks as you head north and look forward to a steady descent down towards the south-east corner of Ponden Reservoir (**B** 996371). Lovers of venerable architecture might enjoy the short detour west along the reservoir to Ponden Hall, a lovely old house, mainly 16th century, and often cited as the model for Emily Brontë's Thrushcross Grange.

The way to the pub is in quite the opposite direction, turning away from the reservoir, east along the water authority roadway, which then becomes the old pre-reservoir road, passing old Ponden Mill (of factory outlet fame) before joining the motor road by a river bridge. There is now a short uphill road walk (but take care: there's no footway and it's quite narrow) of about 250 yards to the 🍺 **Old Silent**. You'll get a decent pint in all of Stanbury's pubs but this free house, in a traditional roadside stone building, has the advantage of being that bit closer! As you'd expect in an out-of-the-way location like this, the place is geared up for food and has a good all-day menu from paninis upwards; but the humble ale drinker is well catered for too. The house beer is from nearby Goose

At the green Peak & Northern footpath sign, keep straight ahead towards Oxenhope, but in another hundred yards join a vehicle track; here, by some silver birch trees, turn right (sign for 'Brontë Falls'). Head straight across the road by a car park and re-enter the open moorland via a wooden kissing gate. The track heads more or less on the level across the moor (watch your footing on this less distinct section). On your right there is the boundary wall of the field intakes, and in about 10 minutes' walking you'll join the much wider track that hugs the side of this wall, still heading west. If it's very wet under-foot, you may prefer to turn right at the road and walk downhill to join this drier wide path straight from the road.

You now have a little over half a mile of walking along the valley as it heads towards the relative wilderness of the high Pennines. Faint hearts may ask 'Where's the pub?', in which case it's a time to steady the nerves maybe by dipping into your flask, although I'd recommend you save this until you get to the river crossing at the so-called Brontë Bridge

Eye, and there are three other mainly local guests in support of the predictable staple, Keighley's Taylor Landlord Bitter. The modernised interior retains a fair bit of character, making this a very welcome halfway house on your walk.

It's a little over a mile to the second rural pub stop on the walk: retrace your route as far as the foot of the hill, where just across the river a signed footpath leaves on the right. After a few yards weaving by the riverside it soon starts a steady climb up the hillside: keep your wits about you for the *bon chemin*, but it's fairly well signed and you'll pass below a house as you climb, before the gradient eases off and you arrive at a metal gate onto a driveway, which leads up to the road above to the left. However, ignore this and continue parallel to the road on the path ('Millennium Way') straight ahead. At the next gate, in Old-field, you're directly below the primary school on the road to your left. Walk up to meet the road at the school and, turning right, walk the short distance along the lane as far as the entrance to Four Fields farm, where a footpath sign points up to the higher road. Be warned, the right of way is to the left of the farm wall as you look at it; and you may have to negotiate a secured gate before walking

up what appears to be a little-used route to join the road on Hare Hill Edge in less than five minutes. The good news is that, even as you emerge on the road, the welcoming sign of the next pub, the **2 Grouse Inn**, is visible just to your right.

The Grouse is efficiently geared up for making the most of its enviable location and extensive views, offering a warm welcome and a very good food menu in a large open-plan building. The four cask ales are all from Timothy Taylor, whose Keighley brewery is probably visible from the huge windows! On entering, there is a small snug aimed at drinkers, though the main room is where to go for the views. This pub is also probably the best place to plump for if you wish to eat a decent plateful on the walk since now the bulk of the route is behind you and most of the remainder is downhill. If I were to complain about anything (not like me of course!), it would be the rather intrusive musak that so many pubs seem to feel they need in order somehow to create atmosphere. (On my visit, the car park was busy and we were probably the only walkers.)

It's about two miles back into Haworth: turn right from the pub and continue along the lane for another 200 yards before turning

Departing Keighley for Haworth on the KWVR

Haworth Old Hall is now a characterful pub and restaurant

into the field by the sign and, keeping on the right of the field boundary, walk down to the lower lane you left at Four Fields Farm. Take care now as the path sign is a little misleading: the right of way is not down the obvious track, but a little to the left first and then down the slope on the left of the boundary fence via Street Head Farm. Keep left before reaching the farm itself on the concrete track; then a waymarker indicates the path on which scenery now rapidly improves as one enters a shady, tree-lined section passing a surprisingly steep drop into a dingly dell on your right. Disregard the signed routes to the side and keep straight ahead into a mini sunken path crossing straight over a farm track and now, following a line of hawthorn trees downhill (there's no trodden track on this stretch so keep the bearing) on a grassy hillside until near the valley bottom, you'll spot a stile next to a metal seven-bar gate; once over this aim for the footbridge and cross the stream on a rather grand bridge.

Now it's fairly plain sailing, although you'll need to gird your loins for the final climb of the day. Walk uphill, bearing round to the right a little into what looks like a small, tree-lined dry valley. This leads up to a wooden ladder stile in front of a farm building. Climb up over this and follow round to the right to walk up a steep farm track to join the motor road by a bus stop (**C** 024373). Now, walk past the Haworth entry sign and the Cemetery Road junction – you'll spot a stone-

flagged footpath on the opposite side of the road, by another bus stop. Cross, and take this path, which leads satisfyingly straight into Haworth village via the Brontë Parsonage, emerging at the top of the steep Main Street.

There are several pubs in Haworth and you may have your own favourites. My two recommendations follow. Halfway down the street on the right is the **3** **Fleece Inn**; the solid stone façade contains a Timothy Taylor House with reliably good ale including the rarer Ram Tam and in winter Taylor's Dark Mild. Like all the pubs on this round, you'll get a good meal here.

Finally, at the foot of the hill where the walk started, the **4** **Haworth Old Hall** is a fine rambling old building, one of the oldest and best in Haworth, with ancient windows and stone mullions aplenty. Once in the main room it's a great place to sit and enjoy a range of beers from the Marston stable, including Ringwood and the very reliable Jennings Bitter and Cumberland Ale. With a bus stop for Keighley right outside and the rail station just across the park, it's also a safe place to linger for that extra pint after a satisfying circuit…

PUB INFORMATION

1 **OLD SILENT**
Hob Lane, Stanbury, BD22 0HW •
01535 647437 • oldsilentinnhaworth.co.uk
Opening hours: 12-11 (midnight Sat; 10.30 Sun)

2 **GROUSE INN**
Harehills Lane, Oldfield, BD22 0RX
01535 643073 • www.thegrouse.co.uk
Opening hours: 11.30-11; 12-10.30 Sun

3 **FLEECE INN**
67 Main Street, Haworth, BD22 8DA •
01535 642172 • fleeceinnhaworth.co.uk
Opening hours: 11-11 (11.30 Fri); 10-11.30 Sat;
10-10.30 Sun

4 **HAWORTH OLD HALL**
8 Sun Street, Haworth, BD22 8BP •
01535 642709 • www.hawortholdhall.co.uk
Opening hours: 12-11 (11.30 Thu-Sat)

The Colne Valley & the 'Huddersfield Narrow'

The Colne Valley is one of Yorkshire's most appealing South Pennine valleys and, like Calderdale, the old mill towns strung along it have reinvented themselves. The once-derelict canal has been brought back to life against the odds. The beer highlight of the walk is the well-known Sair Inn at Linthwaite, former winner of CAMRA's National Pub of the Year award. Its opening hours can be a little erratic. If possible, ring ahead to confirm. Navigation is generally straightforward, but take care to find the right bridleway on Marsden Moor shortly after starting; make use of the map as well as the text. The first pub is a fair hike, especially if going straight to the Sair first: make sure to take some refreshments in your pack, and be aware that the Sair doesn't serve meals.

▶ **Start/finish:** Marsden railway station

▶ **Access:** Trains from West Yorkshire via Huddersfield; or from Manchester

▶ **Distance:** For the complete circuit approx. 8.8 miles (14 km); ending at Slaithwaite: 6.25 miles (10 km)

▶ **OS maps:** Explorer OL21, Explorer 288

▶ **Key attractions:** Classic Pennine valley with old mills and heather moorlands; two brewpubs; restored Huddersfield Narrow' Canal and last 'guillotine' lock

▶ **THE PUBS:** Sair Inn, Linthwaite; Commercial, Shoulder of Mutton, both Slaithwaite; Riverhead Brewery Tap, Marsden

▶ **Timing tips:** Opening hours at the Sair can be erratic; but to find it open at lunchtime do this walk at the weekend. Alternatively, tackle the walk in summer, setting off from Marsden around 2.30pm

The old mill town of Slaithwaite

Wallscape on the path near Slaithwaite

Guillotine lock on the Huddersfield narrow

From Marsden station, cross the canal and head straight down into town arriving via the river and the Riverhead Brewery Tap across the bridge. If you're starting late (or at the weekend) and it's open, my strong recommendation is to resist the Riverhead, otherwise the walk may go west! Save this excellent pub as a reward for completion of the circuit; and instead head right up Peel Street, Marsden's 'main drag', past the striking Institute with its clock tower (now the community centre and library) and crossing the main road as far as the T-junction at the top of Peel Street. Here, bear left and head along the lane (Carrs Road) for another 150 yards taking the footpath on the right just beyond the final house in the terrace. This path heads diagonally up the hillside through the trees: keep on the same broadly eastward trajectory ignoring paths right and left, emerging from the trees and crossing a meadow towards a small cluster of houses just below the open moor. Good views open out as you climb, over Marsden itself and the wider Colne Valley.

KEY

🚶 Walk start/finish

– – – – Walk route

•••••• Alternative route

You'll arrive at a point in the hamlet where a wide untarred lane runs right to left (**A** 057114) just below the open country. Tracks run from here both downhill again to your left and through a gate onto the open moor; ignore these both and instead bear left (close to a decrepit trampoline, which I'm sure will still be there when you read this) along the wide lane, and, after passing a last group of buildings, left, look for a sign pointing

"a sense of well-being grows with every trip to the bar"

THE *GUARDIAN* ON THE SAIR INN, DECEMBER 2008

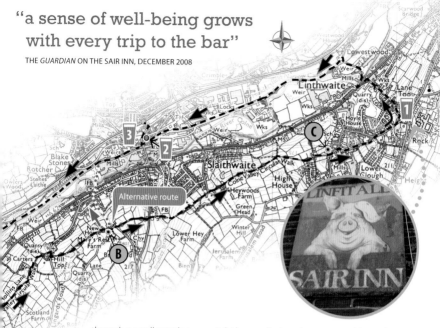

through a small wooden gate on the right that has a National Trust 'Marsden Moor' sign (you may have seen a similar sign back near the old trampoline). If the lane starts going downhill again, you've gone too far! Take the gate (look for the 'Colne Valley Circular Walk' signs from this point, as the next part of the route follows this long-distance route), and head up through the heather for about 75 yards. You'll reach a very good bridleway at right angles, by a small ford immediately left, which you cross, and then continue for almost half a mile on the contour heading broadly NNE, with excellent views across the valley, emerging on the B6107 Meltham Road.

Cross the road to the pavement, turn right, passing the bus stop, and take the path left heading downhill over a stile. Then, passing a plantation on your right, the path bears

Spa Mill chimney, Slaithwaite

right by a well-placed stone seat with a rather enigmatic inscription. The path is now fairly plain sailing for about 300 yards; be careful when climbing over a rickety stile into a sunken track not to be drawn downhill at this point, but to walk uphill for 50 yards and over another stile on the left, following the 'Colne Valley Circular Walk' signs. Again, in a further 50 yards, avoid being drawn downhill; bear right, away from the obvious path, making towards a ruined farmhouse ahead, on the same contour. The track should now be pretty easy to follow as it leads along the hillside with views of Slaithwaite ahead.

At a carefully restored old cottage the path turns into a farm track, and later a tarred lane – Hollins Lane – which brings you out at a junction. Now take care to turn right for a few yards past the house, beyond which the route continues (signed) left across a stone step stile with a wall on your right for a few yards. The path then continues easily for another 500 yards, emerging at another lane (**B** 🕐 077134). This is decision time: either to continue to Linthwaite, whose church spire is now visible ahead (and then later back to Slaithwaite); or to divert down into Slaithwaite first (see box) for some more immediate refreshment. Consult the map and your watch.

If continuing to Linthwaite, the path continues to contour the hillside: head straight across into the short street named Yew Tree and in 50 yards take the signed path ahead. Descend to the main road by a large

house, carefully cross, walk left for 30 yards and double back down the slope. You'll see a small footbridge across the beck below, accessed via a stile and line of telegraph poles through a boggy field; so boggy in fact that you may prefer to make an arc through the next field down to the bridge instead. Then climb back up guided by some marker posts – the path then resumes its progress, passing some cottages and taking you shortly to another lane. Here there's about 100 yards of road walking before the signed route again leaves the road on a sharp right-hand bend and, apart from ducking from one side to the

THE HUDDERSFIELD NARROW CANAL

The Huddersfield Narrow Canal runs 20 miles between Huddersfield and Ashton-under-Lyne. It was conceived as a trans-Pennine link, an alternative to the Rochdale Canal. Apart from the 75 locks required and the height of the central part of the route (at 645 feet the highest in Britain) the main obstacle was at Standedge, west of Marsden, where a three-mile tunnel would be required, the longest in the country at that time. Work on the canal started in 1794, but owing to huge technical problems in the tunnel,

resulting in Thomas Telford being called in as a consultant, the tunnel section wasn't opened until 1811. Shareholders in the project had a torrid time, and even when open the narrow tunnel with no towpath caused huge bottlenecks in traffic. Despite this, the canal had a brief period of prosperity until 1845, when it was bought by the Huddersfield and Manchester Railway Company, and they used the canal to remove spoil from their own tunnel excavations. But once the line was open, the railway

company had no reason to promote the canal, which fell into slow decline and was eventually closed in 1944. In the 30 years before the Huddersfield Canal Society was formed in 1974 with the objective of seeing a re-opening of the canal, all sorts of costly problems obstructed the line of the canal, which had been filled in and built over in some sections. But after 25 years of hard work backed by grants and local council support, the whole canal became navigable once more in May 2001.

Canalside architecture at Slaithwaite

Bar at the Sair, Linthwaite

Commercial, Slaithwaite

other of the boundary wall more than once, is fairly straightforward on its way to Linthwaite. Another path joins from the left and then you head for a new housing estate, crossing one road and then emerging on a second between older stone houses (**C** 095139).

The last stretch before a well-earned reward is on village roads: bear left passing the Methodist church and then fork right at the older chapel ahead, climbing Waingate past a site that was until very recently occupied by large mills, merging with Causeway Side but continuing to climb, until the pavement on the left-hand side peters out (opposite the bus stop), whence fork left (and start downhill again) into Roydhouse Lane, keeping left at the next fork to arrive, at last, at the **Sair Inn**.

Something of a legend, this cosy brewpub was one of the first of its kind and won the CAMRA National Pub of the Year award back in 1997. The quirky atmosphere, the fine and varied ales and the sheer longevity of the place as a pilgrimage for ale lovers is down to veteran landlord Ron Crabtree. The multi-roomed interior has a central corridor and the décor is rustic and welcoming. The house brewery, Linfit, has recently notched up 30 years, and you can

expect to find most of the portfolio of eight beers on sale at any one time. Be careful before sampling the hoppy but strong Old Eli, or even the 6.6% Leadboiler, as the walk is far from over yet. If you do, however, buses are fairly close at hand to rescue you! A real cider from Pure North is also available.

The onward walk to Slaithwaite is, fortunately, very easy. Simply walk down the steep hill (Hoyle Ings) to the main road, cross carefully to the bus stop, and, bearing left as far as Bargate (the road that doubles sharply back to the right in 100 yards or so), drop down here and walk down the road to the canal in a few minutes. Now bear left making use of the towpath to complete the easy mile back into the heart of Slaithwaite. The town once boasted some 14 mills, and has associations with famous woollen firms including Crombie (of the coat). Today a revival is

🚶 DIRECT ROUTE TO SLAITHWAITE

To divert into Slaithwaite from the hillside at point B, simply bear left down the lane and right across the minor road to reach the busy Manchester Road. Cross over carefully, and almost opposite by the bus stop a signed path takes you steeply down steps to cross the River Colne and, via a factory yard, to the canalside towpath right by the curious 'guillotine' lock on the Huddersfield Narrow. Simply walk east (to the right) along the canal for five minutes to emerge right in the heart of Slaithwaite by the Little Bridge bistro and the Commerical inn. Walking on to the Sair at Linthwaite is very simple, reversing the route described in the main text; after which you'll probably be ready for a bus on the Manchester Road.

Shoulder of Mutton, Slaithwaite

Riverhead Brewery Tap, Marsden

underway and, indeed, the former Globe Mills are being transformed into an environmental business centre. Pass the impressive Spa Mills with a very good chimney before arriving right in the town centre via the restored canal wharves, and emerge onto the bridge right opposite the welcoming sight of the  **Commercial**. Since reopening in 2009, this opened-out free house has gone from strength to strength and is now a *Good Beer Guide* regular with nine handpulls offering a wide range of beers including a couple of house beers supplied by the nearby Empire brewery, and a farmhouse cider.

Visible just a few doors further along to the west (don't cross the bridge) is another worthwhile venue, the **3 Shoulder of Mutton**. Another pub that has had its ups and downs, this Punch house has been recently refurbished, retaining some character in its partially opened-out interior layout. It now offers up to six ales, showcasing regional favourites like Copper Dragon and Kelham Island breweries. A simple lunch menu is available until 4pm and may be your best food bet in the pubs on the circuit. Alternatively the Little Bridge bistro across the road right by the bridge is recommended for lunches.

If you wish to call it a day here, public transport is close at hand; but to return to Marsden there are three significant options. Walking, it's a pleasant two-mile stroll along the canal passing almost immediately the Empire brewery on the canalside and, just beyond, the last surviving 'guillotine' lock on the canal. On arrival in Marsden you can make your way back either to the station or, better

still, first to the Riverhead Tap (below). As an alternative to walking, trains to Marsden leave hourly, while buses along the Manchester Road are more frequent.

Back in Marsden, the **4 Riverhead Brewery Tap** by the river and bridge is strongly recommended as a final call, whichever route you choose. Having celebrated its 20th birthday and now owned by Ossett, it nonetheless retains its own in-house brewery serving beers named after local reservoirs. In addition, of course, Ossett beers and other guests make up the 10 ales on tap. Upstairs is a restaurant serving a good range of food and, if you have held out on crisps and nuts until now, this would be the perfect place to indulge yourself. It's only a short stagger to the bus stop or up the hill to the station when the time comes…

PUB INFORMATION

1 SAIR INN
139 Lane Top, Linthwaite, HD7 5SG
01484 842370
Opening hours: 5 (12 Fri & Sat)-11; 12-10.30 Sun

2 COMMERCIAL
1 Carr Lane, Slaithwaite, HD7 5AN
01484 846258 • www.commercial-slaithwaite.co.uk
Opening hours: 12-midnight (1am Fri & Sat)

3 SHOULDER OF MUTTON
9 Church Street, Slaithwaite, HD7 5AS
01484 844661
Opening hours: 12-midnight

4 RIVERHEAD BREWERY TAP
Peel Street, Marsden, HD7 6BR
01484 844324 • www.theriverheadmarsden.co.uk
Opening hours: 12-midnight

The Calder Valley & Wainhouse Tower

For an urban area, close to Halifax and Sowerby Bridge, the landscape here is surprisingly green, and pretty hilly. This pleasant and interesting horseshoe walk takes in some fine hillside woodlands as well as Norland Moor with its summer display of heather and bracken. By contrast there is a little canalside stretch, and the old industrial town of Sowerby Bridge has scrubbed up well in the past 20 years and now sports some very good pubs to finish the day. One of my favourite areas in West Yorkshire to walk. If you want to call it a day at Norland, the 561 bus is available to whisk you back to Halifax.

▶ **Start:** King Cross, Halifax

▶ **Finish:** Sowerby Bridge

▶ **Access:** By rail to Halifax or Sowerby Bridge. Then by bus from Halifax bus station (numerous routes, but 577/578 stops by tower) or Sowerby Bridge town centre (579, 300)

▶ **Distance:** 6.2 miles (10 km) (5 miles omitting the Standard of Freedom)

▶ **OS map:** Explorer OL21

▶ **Key attractions:** Wainhouse Tower; Copley Viaduct and model village; Norland Moor

▶ **THE PUBS:** Standard of Freedom, Skircoat Green; Spring Rock, Greetland; The Works, Puzzle Hall, both Sowerby Bridge. Try also: Firehouse, Navigation, both Sowerby Bridge

▶ **Timing tips:** Do this walk in the summer months to see Norland Moor at its best. The Standard of Freedom opens at noon and the Spring Rock food service stops at 2pm during the week. It's nearly three miles between them.

Woodland path near Greetland

KEY

🚶 Walk start

- - - - Walk route

••••• Alternative route

Alternative route

Alternative route

Alternative route
via road

PUZZLE HALL INN

PUZZLE HALL
INN

🚶 King Cross, which has traffic flying around on some nasty wide roads, is not the ideal place for a walker; but just get off the bus as close as you can to the 250-ft Wainhouse Tower or alight the 577/578 bus alongside the old cemetery on Skircoat Moor Road, just a stone's throw from the junction by the signed path to the tower. Walk a few yards down the path and bear sharp left back to the foot of the tower itself. The folly, as some would call it (see box), stands in a commanding position with a glorious view out across the Calder Valley, an iconic West

Yorkshire landscape with Sowerby Bridge occupying the valley floor below. Walk on past the tower and cross the lane into Delph Hill Road. After 100 yards veer left into Rose Terrace, keeping the terrace of four cottages on your right. At the end of the houses a footpath rises through some scrub for a short distance, emerging on a narrow lane of stone setts; turn downhill again towards some woodland. Reaching this, the path turns sharply right but two earthen paths run off before you into Scarr Wood. Take the lower of these, which leads directly downhill to a road junction in a few minutes.

Directly across in the same direction you'll see a path continuing into the woods.

Standard of Freedom, Skircoat Green

Follow this into pleasant Long Wood, keeping to the obvious path heading gently downhill; but if you're omitting the first pub, see the box below for alternative directions. Just before the point where the path appears to disgorge you into a modern housing estate, take a path on the left, which climbs up and emerges into a lane – New Road – at the top corner of the woodland. From here it's a five-minute walk along the quiet lane, which leads directly to the 🗍 **Standard of Freedom** at Skircoat Green, an old weaving hamlet at the southern edge of Halifax today.

The pub has been opened out and modernised, but the great view from the window seat across the valley is as good as you're likely to get from any pub in this book. Maybe a quick half here as there's much to do yet; the three beers are Black Sheep Bitter, Taylor Landlord and Tetley Cask, badged here as the house beer.

Coming out of the pub, turn right, and a few yards along take the steps right, down to Lower Skircoat Green Road. Directly across the road, an alley, 'The Scarr', snakes down between the hillside stone cottages. Work your way down to the lowest path, marked by a solid stone wall; head to the left on this wider track – Cow Lane – which runs down

towards the railway, leading under the line and disgorging you onto the busy Wakefield Road at the bottom. Taking care, turn right and look for the path on the opposite side in a few yards, crossing the canal almost immediately. Drop down to the towpath here and walk westwards (same direction as on the road) as far as Copley Lane Bridge, the next bridge, and walk down into Copley under the rail bridge. Copley is a small 'model village' of a few terraces founded by mill-owner and philanthropist Edward Akroyd in the 1840s. Akroyd went on to build a far larger model community closer to Halifax named Akroydon, and helped his workers save money to buy their own homes. The handsome gothic-style buildings both there and here at Copley survive today, although the large mill Akroyd built has gone. Copley is now a Conservation Area.

Keep straight ahead beyond the bus turning circle (**B** 🕑 085224) and cross the river bridge by the surprisingly large church and the pretty little toll gate, which suggests this trackway was once an important route. Climb steadily into the woodland, passing a white house; and as the trees thin out a fine view opens up of the impressive Copley rail viaduct and the Wainhouse Tower, which is rarely out of view henceforth. Follow the path down past the large cluster of farm buildings and on to a smaller building; just

The route climbs alongside pretty Maple Dean Clough

Toll House at Copley

beyond here at a clear path junction, bear left and climb uphill into the trees, passing under telegraph wires, and ignoring a good path joining from the left. Soon the path follows a fence that joins on the right, and you're heading for a deep clough occupied by a small stream. Upon reaching this, follow the track, keeping close to the stream – uphill fairly strenuously for a few minutes – to emerge via a stone step stile onto a junction of lanes at the edge of Norland Moor (C 🕑 070220).

THE WAINHOUSE TOWER

The 250-ft Wainhouse Tower was named after John Wainhouse, who owned a nearby dyeworks. He conceived the chimney to reduce pollution from the works; but having commissioned a local architect to beautify the top section with its balcony and elaborate lantern dome, and having it opened in 1875 at a cost of £15,000, it was never used for its original purpose and Wainhouse died shortly afterwards. After passing through several private owners, in 1918 the Halifax Courier organised a public subscription in order for the Halifax Corporation to purchase the structure, in whose hands it has been ever since. It is occasionally open to the public – but be warned, there are 403 steps to the top!

Look right, and just before the boundary sign for Norland you'll see a wide track heading out onto the heath (if time is pressing, the quickest way to the Spring Rock is to take the Norland Road running away to the left and keep going; about half a mile). Walk up this path as far as the mini-pylon and bear hard left on the Calderdale Way on a good track. In summer the moor has a feel of a lowland heath more like Dorset or Surrey than the Pennines. Keep to this path at the edge of the heath for about 10 minutes, passing first a well-made conical cairn (bear left here), then a farmhouse on your left and reaching a path crossing before a second cairn. Take the less distinct left-hand option to the stile in the boundary and then follow the field edge down to a good farm track and keep ahead to the cluster of buildings including the 2 **Spring Rock** in front of you. This welcoming stone-built pub has had a sympathetic makeover inside, aided by a woodburning stove in each of the two main rooms, floorboards and chunky tables. Five handpumps dispense a changing range of well-kept beers. This is the obvious place to break for food on the walk, and there's a tempting menu with options to suit most appetites;

but, again, be warned that during the week, including Fridays, there is no food service between 2pm and 5pm.

Assuming you've no need of the bus back to Halifax from outside the pub, retrace your steps to Norland Moor, remembering to veer off the farm track by the gate and before the house. This time head straight across at the path crossing beyond the stile, and keep ahead on the good track on the same bearing right across Norland Moor until you approach a loose-knit group of buildings that is the hamlet of Norland Town, reaching the road by a car park and children's playground.

Bear right and walk straight across at the junction, passing the primary school on your left and church on your right (Bury Moor Road). Merge into Norland Town Road and walk downhill passing a handsome old yeoman's house on the left. Immediately before Upper Old Hall, just past the former Blue Ball pub, turn left, and you'll see a stile by a gate (FP sign). Head over here and walk to the next stile ahead. A fine panorama over Sowerby Bridge opens up before you.

The path is indistinct here: ignore the obvious track ahead past some odd standing slates, and instead head at 45 degrees down to the right, aiming for the far corner of the next field, picking up a gate stile. Now obey the sign and follow the field boundary downhill and then left, bringing you to a step stile in the corner (**D** 🕾 065233). Drop down to join the small lane, and bear left. Just beyond the row of houses in 100 yards, an unsigned but obvious path leads off to the right, a pleasant walled path with stone setts underfoot. Excellent views over the old centre of Sowerby Bridge lie right below you as you swing round and down a steep bank to emerge on a small terrace of houses and, just beyond, a road junction. All downhill roads here lead to the town centre. I suggest straight across, then turn right steeply down and right again over the River Ryburn bridge to emerge on the A58 next to the railway bridge. A well-earned beer is close at hand. Under the rail bridge turn left into Hollins Mill Lane at the Firehouse (see below), and a few yards on the right is **3** **The Works**.

Wainhouse Tower, from Norland

An imaginative conversion of an old foundry, this is one of several new and refurbished bars that have helped put this old mill town on the beer map. The welcoming and spacious interior offers a range of 'seating experiences' and an excellent menu of everything from sandwiches to big meals to complement the ales on offer. Expect three Timothy Taylor ales, a good range of rotating guests and real ciders on more than a dozen handpumps.

Leaving The Works, head further down Hollins Mill Lane, which runs between the River Calder to your left and the Rochdale Canal on the embankment up to your right. The **4 Puzzle Hall** comes into view soon on the left, a quirky and venerable old architectural confection, the result in part of once having a small tower brewery inside. The bare room on entry is a venue for local bands; walk through to the cosy little room by the bar, warmed when needed by a real fire, to find a changing range of up to six ales. If you're a Thai food aficionado, save your appetite for here as Thai food is served from 5pm except on Monday and Tuesday.

There are other good drinking options in town if you're still game: try the **5 Firehouse**, which you passed earlier; it's mainly an eatery but has two or three well-kept beers on tap; or, for a more pubby alternative, head down to the **6 Navigation** by the canal on Chapel Lane (off main A58)

Inside the Spring Rock

SHORT-CUT TO COPLEY OMITTING THE STANDARD OF FREEDOM

If you're in a hurry (perhaps to reach the Spring Rock in good time for lunch), take this alternative route to save about a mile. In Long Wood look for a smaller path about 100 yards in (**A** 083233) which runs off the main path on the right at about 45 degrees. It leads down steadily towards the lower wall of the woods and a row of back gardens beyond. At the foot of the slope you should see a small path running between two gardens. This brings you out onto the busy Wakefield Road. Walk back until you reach the bus stop a couple of hundred yards away, and directly opposite a path leads down to the canal. Cross this on the bridge and follow the path that bears left under the end of the impressive Copley Viaduct and across to emerge on one of Copley's two parallel streets of model workers' housing. At the far end pick up the main route at point B (see main text).

at the eastern end of town, with beers from Yorkshire brewers great and small.

The railway station is well signed and close to the town centre for getting home.

PUB INFORMATION

1 STANDARD OF FREEDOM
2 New Lane, Skircoat Green, HX3 0TE
01422 322664 • www.standardoffreedom.co.uk
Opening hours: 12-11

2 SPRING ROCK
Norland Road, Greetland, HX4 8PT
01422 377722
Opening hours: 12-11

3 THE WORKS
12 Hollins Mill Lane, Sowerby Bridge, HX6 2QG
01422 834821 • www.theworkssowerbybridge.co.uk
Opening hours: 12-11; 12-10.30 Sun

4 PUZZLE HALL
21 Hollins Mill Lane, Sowerby Bridge, HX6 2RF
01422 835547 • www.puzzlehall.com
Opening hours: 4-midnight (1am Fri); 1-1am Sat;
1-midnight Sun

Try also:

5 FIREHOUSE
1 Town Hall Street, Sowerby Bridge, HX6 2QD
01422 832586 • firehouserestaurant.co.uk
Opening hours: closed Mon; 4 (12 Sat)-11.30;
12-10.30 Sun

6 NAVIGATION
Chapel Lane, Sowerby Bridge, HX6 3LF
01422 316073 • www.thenavigationpub.co.uk
Opening hours: closed Mon; 12-3, 5-11 Tue-Fri;
12-11 Sat & Sun

Canals & mills: Halifax to Brighouse

Halifax is probably my favourite of the larger Pennine mill towns. It has suffered less than most others from insensitive modern development, and the hilly, well-wooded landscape in the area around it offers fine walking with great views. This is one such walk: you climb quite steeply out of town with an extensive panorama, returning along a pleasant reach of the canal leading back to Elland with the option of a further hillside stretch back into two fine Halifax hostelries. Later detours by bus or on foot are best planned ahead, and the tourist office in Halifax can supply details of the Hebble Trail.

▶ **Start/finish:** Halifax railway station

▶ **Access:** Frequent trains from Manchester, Leeds and Bradford

▶ **Distance:** 9.5 miles (15 km) for complete circuit (4 miles to Red Rooster)

▶ **OS map:** Explorer 288

▶ **Key attractions:** Piece Hall; Hebble Trail; Calder & Hebble Navigation

▶ **THE PUBS:** Shoulder of Mutton, Southowram; Red Rooster, Brookfoot; Barge & Barrel, Elland; Cross Keys, Siddal; Three Pigeons, Halifax

▶ **Timing tips:** Save this walk for a weekend on account of the lunchtime closure of the first two pubs. At the weekend the Shoulder of Mutton opens at midday so plan accordingly. If you want to abort *en route*, check bus times before setting out!

Barge & Barrel on the Calder and Hebble Navigation

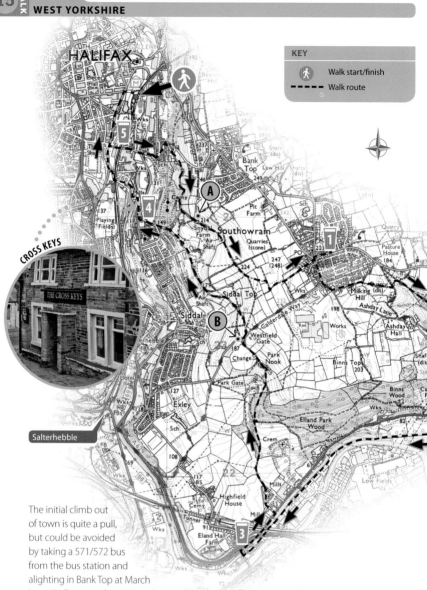

KEY

🚶 Walk start/finish

– – – – Walk route

CROSS KEYS

THE CROSS KEYS

Salterhebble

The initial climb out
of town is quite a pull,
but could be avoided
by taking a 571/572 bus
from the bus station and
alighting in Bank Top at March
Lane. Walk up another 100 yards
or so and bear right into Dog Kennel Lane
by the conifer tree, and keep going on the
same trajectory past the radio mast to join
the route at point A in the text. One warning:
unusually these days you will struggle to find
much to eat at any of these pubs, so, if you're
making a day of this walk, I strongly recommended you take your own food and find a
good spot to eat al fresco….

🚶 From Halifax station the walk heads
south along Church Street – although
you can also take the steps down to the
Eureka theme museum alongside the station
and walk right through the car park to emerge
by the Three Pigeons (see below). Time permitting, a visit to the wonderful Piece Hall is
recommended (see box). This early industrial
treasure is at last enjoying the recognition it
deserves after decades of neglect.

Just beyond the Three Pigeons – to which you'll be returning later in the day – turn left down Water Lane and under the rail bridge. Now carry on uphill towards the cemetery, where the main road to Siddal bears right. Keep going past Stoney Royd cemetery and bear right onto Trooper Lane, with good views opening up over Halifax as you climb. The road twists and turns – this is not an ascent for the faint hearted! At a point where

Shoulder of Mutton, Southowram

Continue ahead past the houses (keeping them on your left) on a path contouring along the hillside into open country. Cross a wide, grassy bridleway after a few minutes, and keep ahead. You'll see in the field ahead a grassy path climbing the field towards a gap in the wall. Once through the next stile, bear uphill on this path, which quickly leads you to the brow of the hill and a near-360-degree panorama. Go to the far top corner of the field and bear right along the wall through the next field before swinging left through a stile, and walk down towards the village of Southowram, whose outskirts are visible ahead. Merge with a track and emerge in the village centre on a road junction. The **1 Shoulder of Mutton** with its visible pub sign is some 150 yards ahead, and in summer the stone exterior will probably be covered in a fine floral display. Inside, the L-shaped lounge (there's a separate public room with a pool table) has an open fire. Expect a Saltaire beer (usually Blonde) and changing guests.

On leaving the pub, retrace your steps to the road junction; bear left down the road past the general store and downhill past the bus stops to reach and turn down School Lane on your left. At the end of this street continue down a narrow path between modern houses, with a rather handsome church tower directly ahead.

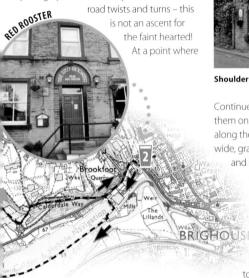

you reach a cobbled street, High Grove Lane, where Trooper Lane turns left, keep going ahead on High Grove Lane. The striking, modern, triangular building in the town centre is the HQ of the Halifax Building Society, completed in the early 1970s, while the other noteworthy sight in the panorama is the Wainhouse Tower (see Walk 14), the chimney-turned-folly that dominates the Calder Valley away to your right. The lane peters out into a very attractive cobbled path, which levels out for a while between stone walls lined with mature trees and shrubs. If you're on the right path, you'll pass under a radio mast. At a path junction, bear left and start climbing again.

At the top of the pull emerge by a pair of houses marked 'Snydal Farm' on the map (A 🧭 102240) with a road running back up to the radio mast to your sharp left and a fine panorama across Halifax to your right.

THE PIECE HALL

Completed in 1779, Halifax Piece Hall was built as a trading hall for locally made, hand-woven 'pieces' of woollen cloth. These were brought by packhorse from the homes of handloom weavers in Calderdale and beyond. With its classical colonnades and its great courtyard, it was the most prestigious cloth hall of its kind in the country; and when industrialisation and the factory system made this function redundant, the Hall survived to be used for other functions, notably as a wholesale market for the Halifax Corporation. The Piece Hall is now the only surviving cloth hall in Britain. In 1928 it became the first commercial/industrial building to be scheduled as an Ancient Monument, and it went on to be Grade I listed in 1954. English Heritage has called it 'perhaps Yorkshire's most important secular building'. It has been somewhat neglected for many years but should by the time you read this have re-opened as a shopping, heritage and leisure venue. One can only hope the gravitas of this wonderful building is not compromised by undue commercialisation.

Leave Southowram behind and return to open country. Keep to the obvious path with the wall on your left as you head downhill towards a wooded valley. The landmark on the horizon will be familiar to many: the TV mast on Emley Moor which opened up TV reception to the north in the early 1950s. We're now walking on part of the Calderdale Way, one of my favourite long-distance paths. At the foot of the field, bear right onto a wide earthen lane – but only for a few yards – before dropping down left on a signed path into the clough below. Follow it through the wall and round across the stream and uphill on a path composed of excellent stone setts up to a signed path junction in 50 yards. Here, bear sharp right ('Cromwell Bottom').

Now you have a pleasant stroll of over half a mile downhill through pretty Cromwell Wood. Emerge into fields with the main Brighouse–Elland Road close by below you. Just beyond is Brookfoot Lake. As you pass a farm building on the right, look out for steps to a gate on the left; take this and climb steadily for a short way until you reach the pylons and a junction of paths. Bear right on the Calderdale Way and

follow this, another good wide track, which brings you out directly to the main road. Bear left on the pavement: it's not a pleasant road to walk along but it's mercifully short, and as you round the corner beyond the road to Southowram you'll see the **7 Red Rooster** on the roadside at a sharp corner.

One of the first of a new generation of alehouses, the Rooster is by now a long-standing fixture in the Calderdale ale scene. It offers, alongside regulars from the likes of Timothy Taylor and Saltaire, a wide range of guest beers to tempt the palate, including dark ales. Gentlemen lovers of real urinals (not the modern imposters) will wish to pay a visit here – Oates & Green, of course (see below)!

It's about two miles to the Barge & Barrel along a canal path. Buses are very scarce, so taking a cab might be the best option if you want to avoid the walk. For hardy souls doing things the proper way, leave the pub and walk back along the road as far as a point opposite the path you walked down from the Cromwell Wood and take the signed path by the bus stop down to the canal towpath by a derelict old lockkeeper's cottage. Now a pleasant backwater, the navigation was completed in the 1860s to connect the Aire & Calder Navigation at Wakefield with Halifax and the Rochdale canal at Sowerby Bridge. Unlike many other canals it has remained open for navigation ever since it was built. Turn right along the canal and, although it's only a short distance from the main road, it's a pleasant stroll along the towpath for the best part of two miles past Cromwell Nature Reserve as far as Elland Bridge.

You will have passed the **3** **Barge & Barrel**, the second canalside pub on the opposite bank, just yards earlier, so it's a very short walk back once over the bridge. Despite the less-than-sylvan location right alongside a pair of busy roads, once inside this solid Victorian pub this aspect of the modern world is put behind you. Ironically it's here because it once served another form of transport: the old Elland railway station was close by. A spacious, opened-out interior formed from several once-separate rooms makes up the main drinking area wrapping around the servery. Like the Red Rooster, the Barge & Barrel is a well-known and long-standing alehouse that has built a good reputation for serving a wide range of well-kept beers at keen prices; and, alongside old favourites like Abbeydale Moonshine, Black Sheep Bitter and Timothy Taylor's Landlord, you'll find several guests, primarily from local micros. The lunchtime food cut-off at 2pm is probably too early for most – unless you're running the course!

Before leaving this *Good Beer Guide* regular, you'll need to consider your next move. The 'official' route takes you over the shoulder of the hill back into Halifax, but there are alternatives for the less hardy: you may have had enough walking by now, in which case it's possible to catch a bus (perhaps the infrequent 537 service, which drops you near the Three Pigeons) or book a cab; a less strenuous walking alternative is to follow the canal to Salterhebble then the interesting and waymarked Hebble Trail up into Halifax.

That leaves the hardy walkers to head right out of the pub and under the road bridge, crossing the Brighouse Road carefully. By the next bus stop in 200 yards or so turn left up a side road, which leads straight up, passing a terrace of houses, and narrows to a wide brick-lined track that leads back into open country and uphill into the edge of Elland Park Wood, the tree-covered hillside ahead. Keep your eyes out for a point, some 10 minutes further on and well into the trees, where another track leads off right. (If you reach a path leading off to the left, you have gone too far!) Turn here, and just 10 yards along this a third path, narrower but well defined nonetheless, leads left uphill. This is the path we want, and it leads pleasantly uphill with views down on your left to the lower track you have recently left, as that path leads into a tiny hamlet below you. Keep on this path across another and then through a gate, which on the same course climbs up to a group of stone cottages,

Climbing Trooper Lane will reward you with fine views of Halifax

emerging into the end of an unadopted lane, which you follow (more on the level now!) to arrive at a tarred road (**B** 106231).

It's plain sailing now. Cross more or less straight over onto another unadopted lane and follow this, with good views out across the small Hebble Valley, running down from Halifax to the Calder. The lane leads downhill into a copse and then passes the remains of White Gate brickworks, with two chimneys having so far survived demolition. Follow downhill onto a steepening and now cobbled road, but note the blue plaque to the famous historian E.P. Thompson on the house opposite the cemetery. It was here that Thompson wrote his seminal work *The Making of the English Working Class*.

At the foot of the lane by the main road junction stands the **4** **Cross Keys**. Arguably the most improved pub in Calderdale, its enthusiastic and competent new licensees have, in a short space of time, transformed this once-nondescript three-roomed local into a popular and successful destination and won a handful of CAMRA awards. Expect a friendly welcome, a real fire in winter, and up to six well-kept beers (and a changing real cider) on handpump. Gratifyingly, the gents contains a fine set of original Oates & Green 'real' urinals, manufactured right here in Halifax!

Across the road, buses leave frequently to take you back into Halifax if you wish, but in fact it's only a short and atmospheric walk now to your final pub and, beyond it, the town centre. Take the curiously named Boys Lane, which runs downhill almost opposite the pub, to cross the Hebble Brook and the canal before passing under the shadow of the great Shaw Lodge Mill with its towering chimney, and the Shears Inn (which you could add to your itinerary: far more atmospheric outside than in, and majoring on Taylor beers) before climbing

Three Pigeons, Halifax

up to the railway bridge. Bear right here to join the main road, and now it's just five minutes' walk to the final stop of the day, the **5** **Three Pigeons**. Several years of TLC by the current owner, Ossett brewery (which won a conservation award for its work in 2006), have enhanced the distinctive character of this fine early 1930s pub. Unassuming from the outside, the interior is a revelation, containing some superb art deco styling in the door signage, wood panelling and terrazzo flooring. The octagonal drinking lobby, from which most of the many rooms radiate, is thought to be unique. Beer choice is far better than in its Websters' days, and in addition to Ossett's (mostly very blonde) offerings you can expect several guests. An excellent pub to end the day, and it's just a short walk up to the station and the town centre.

PUB INFORMATION

1 **SHOULDER OF MUTTON**
14 Cain Lane, Southowram, HX3 9SB
07926 625195
Opening hours: 2-11; 12-midnight Fri & Sat

2 **RED ROOSTER**
123 Elland Road, Brookfoot, Brighouse, HD6 2QR
01484 713737
Opening hours: 4-11; 12-midnight Fri & Sat;
12-10.30 Sun

3 **BARGE & BARREL**
10-20 Park Road, Elland, HX5 9HP
01422 371770
Opening hours: 12-11.30

4 **CROSS KEYS**
3 Whitegate, Siddal, HX3 9AE
01422 300348
Opening hours: 3-11; 12-11 Fri-Sun

5 **THREE PIGEONS**
1 Sun Fold, Halifax, HX1 2LX
01422 347001 • www.ossett-brewery.co.uk/pubs/
three-pigeons-halifax
Opening hours: 4-11; 12-11 Fri-Sun

Ilkley Moor & the Dales Way

WALK 16

It's a safe bet that only a tiny fraction of the people who know the famous song about Ilkley Moor have ventured onto it; this varied and generally easy walk offers an opportunity to put that right, though technically much of the moorland stretch is on Addingham Moor adjacent. A steep initial climb on roads (which could be avoided, if you wish, by a short cab ride) is followed by a level moorland edge, offering easy walking with extensive views before the descent to Addingham. Addingham had its moment in the sun during the 2014 Yorkshire stages of the Tour de France, being the only place to feature on both stages. It also offers a choice of good places to eat and drink before the return to Ilkley, which is a pleasant, easy stroll along the Wharfe on the Dales Way. Only the last stretch down into Addingham is likely to present any navigational challenges, but the moorland stretch reaches 1200 feet and might be best left for a fine day.

- **Start/finish:** Ilkley railway station
- **Access:** Frequent trains from Leeds and Bradford
- **Distance:** 9.7 miles (15.6 km)
- **OS map:** Explorer 297
- **Key attractions:** Ilkley Moor; Addingham village; Dales Way riverside path; Bolton Abbey (www.bolton-abbey.com; 4 miles)
- **THE PUBS:** Swan, Crown, both Addingham; Crescent Inn, Bar T'at, both Ilkley. Try also: Fleece, Addingham
- **Timing tips:** The Swan at Addingham is closed at lunchtimes except at weekends. Allow up to three hours for a leisurely walk from Ilkley to Addingham.

Wharfedale from the Swastika Stone, Ilkley Moor

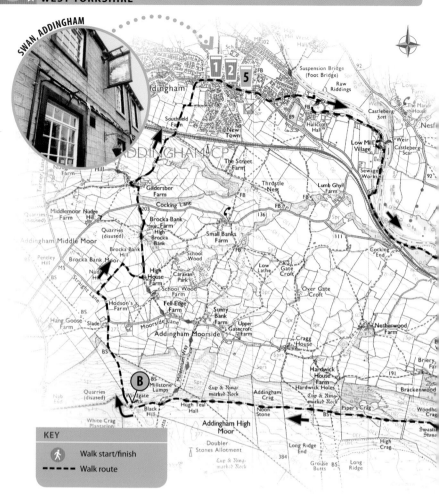

SWAN, ADDINGHAM

KEY

👤 Walk start/finish

- - - - - Walk route

👤 Ilkley's rail and bus stations are adjacent each other opposite the imposing Town Hall, and this makes the natural place to start. Part of the old Victorian station has been colonised by coffee shops should you wish to fortify yourself before the climb ahead; but as suggested above, should you feel disinclined to tackle the steady pull up Wells Road opposite, you could summon a cab to take you up to the moor edge by the Millennium Way path on the Keighley Road, making sure to alight by the car park 200 yards after the left turn off the Wells Road (point A on the map).

If you're doing it properly, Wells Road is across from the station, leading up the hill. Keep straight ahead past some attractive stone buildings, and follow the road over a cattle grid as it curves to the right. Already you're in semi-open country with the skyline of Ilkley Moor on the left. Pass Darwin Gardens on your right. Charles Darwin came to Ilkley in 1859 to undergo hydropathy ('the water-cure') at the Wells House Hydropathic Establishment (this is the imposing mansion, now apartments, just beyond the gardens). While Darwin was in Ilkley, his chef d'oeuvre *On the Origin of Species* was first published.

The Victorian station buildings in Ilkley

In the Crown at Addingham

down Hebers Ghyll, a local beauty spot. Disregard this, however, and continue ahead keeping the wall on your right; but watch your footing on this stretch as in summer bracken can almost obscure the paths as they wind through this section. As long as you keep more or less on the contour, you won't go far wrong, and very soon you'll emerge from the vegetation and see ahead the fenced outcrop of Woodhouse Crag, which you should aim for. There's also a tremendous view across Lower Wharfedale which you'll enjoy the more if you have earned it by walking up the hill from Ilkley! The fence protects the famous carved Swastika Stone – nothing to do with the Nazis, as the Swastika was used as a religious symbol long before their time, and this rock carving, one of many on the Moor, is likely to date back to circa 2000 BC.

Beyond the stone the path is an easy, pleasant walk, gradually uphill, for about a mile and a half, through a number of gates, until eventually a view opens out across to the left, past a mast, and down towards Keighley. Not far beyond this you'll arrive at a prominent cairn, where a green and yellow waymark points down to the right through the heather. In bad weather you can escape downhill here, but otherwise I recommend

Further along, at Westwood House – another large Victorian pile – bear left into Keighley Road by the thoughtfully placed bench. This 300-yard stretch is the steepest of the day, but as it levels off, look out for a signed footpath striking off on the right just before a car park (**A** 🅿 111468). Now follow this prominent path, part of the Millennium Way, as it skirts the edge of Ilkley Moor with substantial houses over the wall on your right. The path climbs very gently but steadily, passing a small enclosed reservoir on the right, and beyond, entering a wooded clough, where you'll pass a path striking off through a gate on the right continuing just five minutes or so further, onto the top of Black Hill, and just before the trees of White Crag Plantation, where at Windgate Nick (**B** 🕐 069471) there's a bench and a memorial to two airmen who died when their de Havilland Mosquito crashed nearby in 1943. If it's warm enough, you can pause to enjoy the view and maybe take some refreshments if you've brought some; now it's downhill, following the partly worn route in the grass directly from the bench towards the straight wall that runs down towards the lower farmland; but always keeping well to the right of the wall before the path leads through an open gateway and then down to the farmhouse below, where you emerge on a bend of a quiet rural lane.

Bar counter at the Fleece

Now follow the lane left as far as the signed footpath that leads down a farm track by a collection of mailboxes. Follow this track as it bears round 90 degrees right through a gate towards a stone farmhouse. Now, just before you swing into the farmyard with the friendly 'Keep Out' sign and maybe a chained guard dog on duty, locate a stone step stile in the left-hand wall leading into a small paddock; there's then another similar stile in the far corner, leading into a larger field. Simply follow the line of telegraph poles leading downhill, merging with a wider rough track, crossing the quiet Cocking Lane and heading up to the farm hamlet at Gildersber just beyond. At the farm, the way you want goes straight through the farmyard and out the far end, but perversely the actual right of way doesn't. To obey the letter of the law, bear left, and then right in 15 yards (waymark), disregard the house gate in front of you, instead bearing slightly left to curve round the back of the buildings in front of you and over a signed step stile in the far right corner of the small paddock, through a gate, and emerging on a dung-bestrewn road about

20 yards from the point you started the manoeuvre!

In consultation with your map the rest is now easy: through the metal gate in front, pass some asbestos farm buildings and follow the signed farm track downhill (forking left about 150 yards beyond where the waymark has become indistinct), with great views ahead, marred only slightly by the increasing sound from the bypass road below. Close to the road, take care to find the kissing gate in a gap in the hedge to emerge on the edge of the busy road. WARNING: The A65 bypass road here is fast and fairly busy, although sight lines are very good. Be patient and wait for a good gap in the traffic before attempting to cross. Safely across, keep straight down the field (ignore the other right of way signed to the left) with the hedge on your right, and locate the waymark at the foot of the field leading right into a little sunken lane. Follow this for 50 yards, then take the step stile to the left by the large oak tree. Now follow the wall down into the village, crossing a tiny beck before emerging onto the village main street, with the pub sign of the **1** **Swan** visible 150 yards down to your right by the crossing. As stated earlier this will only be open at the weekend, unless you have set out very late.

This substantial friendly village local retains a four-room layout arranged around a small central stone-flagged bar. Don't miss the cosy little snug to the left of the bar and the wonderful old range, which may be original, in the more opened-out area to the right. At least four cask ales are always available with a strong LocAle focus: Ilkley Mary Jane and Copper Dragon Best Bitter are regulars, and Ilkley Black is a frequent guest.

A little further down the road, on the junction with the 'B' road to Bolton Abbey, stands the **2** **Crown**. It's another multi-room pub with enough of its historic layout remaining to qualify for inclusion in *Yorkshire's Real Heritage Pubs*. The right-hand side of the pub has the two notable rooms: the front snug has match-board-backed seating and a simple fireplace, whilst beyond an old cross passage the rear smoke room, now the games room, has fitted seating, a boarded ceiling, a service hatch and an old enamel door sign. The pub

RAF memorial, Addingham Moor

offers Goose Eye's Chinook Blonde alongside the now Wolverhampton-brewed Tetley Bitter as regulars, and a couple of guests from the likes of Goose Eye, Wharfedale or Ossett. Food is largely of the pie variety (check the website for details). If you're after food of a different sort and/or are just game for an extra stop before leaving Addingham, you would do well to try the

5 Fleece just another 75 yards down the main street. The pub majors on food, but with four reliable beers from Yorkshire breweries to wash it down – including the excellent Sal-taire Blonde and, very frequently, the popular local hero Ilkley Mary Jane – in a traditional

two-roomed interior, it's a very good addition, particularly if the Swan is shut.

The time has come for the saunter back to Ilkley, but it's a gentle and pleasant stroll, mainly on the riverside. Continue about 300 yards beyond the Fleece and bear off left at about 45 degrees by the Co-op at the road junction onto Church Street, at the end of which there's a signed path opposite running between houses down towards the church itself, but also doubling as the Dales Way path to Ilkley. Follow the well-marked path as it heads down to the churchyard (keep the church on your left and look for waymarks leading right to join the quiet, wooded Low Mill Lane). Turn left. It's a lovely walk along this tree-shaded backwater towards the eponymous little industrial hamlet adjacent the weir on the Wharfe and opposite the limestone outcrop of Castleberg Scar, above which is an ancient hill fort, not visible from the walk. Once through the hamlet, the path follows Old Lane and merges with the old Ilkley Road,

The path on Ilkley Moor is generally level and easy

now mercifully bypassed by the nearby A65, before leading back down to a pretty riverside path. It's a little under two miles from here into the centre of Ilkley, and the Dales Way is well signed all the way so you should be able to switch to auto-pilot and enjoy the walk. Pass the town's picturesque old bridge, which is technically the start (or end) of the Dales Way, and continue through Ilkley Park to the modern bridge on New Brook Street. Here, turn right to head up into the town centre. You won't miss the Crescent Hotel on the main cross roads five minutes further on, an imposing Victorian building that sweeps gracefully around the south-east corner of the junction. The **3 Crescent Inn** occupies a ground-floor corner of the hotel and, since its refurbishment five years ago, has become a real ale destination, offering eight cask beers. The house ale is produced by Ilkley brewery, but the guests are rarely from too far away either. There's always plenty of food if you need it, but try to save a bit of space for one more contrasting venue. To reach it, simply head west down busy Church Street and take the second left into Cunliffe Road. Some way up on the left is the **4 Bar T'at**, a cheerful conversion of a former shop. It has built up a good reputation for both its beer and food (the latter mainly available in its basement restaurant). Beer-wise expect some interesting and eclectic guests

PUB INFORMATION

1 SWAN
106 Main Street, Addingham, LS29 0NS
01943 831999 • www.swan-addingham.co.uk
Opening hours: 5.30-11 Mon-Thu; 5-11 Fri;
12-midnight Sat; 12-10.30 Sun

2 CROWN
136 Main Street, Addingham, LS29 0NS •
01943 830278 • www.thecrowninnaddingham.co.uk
Opening hours: 12-midnight Mon-Thu; 12-1am
Fri & Sat; 12-10.30 Sun

3 CRESCENT INN
Brook Street, Ilkley, LS29 8DG
01943 811250
Opening hours: 12-11 Mon-Wed; 12-midnight Thu-
Sat; 12-11 Sun

4 BAR T'AT
7 Cunliffe Road, Ilkley, LS29 9DZ
01943 608888 • www.mttbartat.co.uk
Opening hours: 12-2.30, 5.30-9 Mon-Fri;
12-9 Sat; 12-6 Sun

Try also:

5 FLEECE
154 Main Street, Addingham, LS29 0LY
01943 830491 • www.fleeceinnaddingham.co.uk
Opening hours: 12-10.30 (midnight Fri & Sat)

alongside solid Yorkshire favourites. Check the pub's Twitter page (@Bar_Tat) to get a flavour of what's coming up. Continuing to the top of Cunliffe Road and turning left will quickly return you to the station.

Crescent Inn,
Ilkley

Harden Beck & Goitstock from Bingley

There's plenty of interest in this woodland walk along the Harden Beck, a beauty spot accessed directly from Bingley town centre. Evidence of former water-powered industry abounds along the stream before you reach one of the scenic highlights of the route, the impressive Hewenden Viaduct, once part of a rail line known as the 'Alpine route'. From the ale taster's perspective the highlight must surely be the George at Cullingworth, a popular and award-winning community local. An alternative option from here, rather than returning to Bingley, is to walk on to Cross Roads for Haworth and link in with walk 12, if you're staying in the area for longer. Wear stout footwear as the path through Goitstock Wood can be muddy; navigation is fairly straightforward.

▶ **Start/finish:** Bingley railway station

▶ **Access:** 20 minutes from Leeds or Bradford by rail

▶ **Distance:** 9 miles (14.5 km); 4.8 miles to the George at Cullingworth

▶ **OS maps:** Explorer OL21, Explorer 288

▶ **Key attractions:** Bingley lock flight, Leeds & Liverpool canal; Goit Stock woods and waterfall; Hewenden and Cullingworth Viaducts; Great Northern Railway Trail

▶ **THE PUBS:** Malt, Harden; George, Cullingworth; Foundry Hill, Bingley. Try also: Potting Shed, Bingley

▶ **Timing tip:** The Malt opens at 11.30 daily allowing a prompt start from Bingley

Hewenden Viaduct is one of the highlights of the route

Bingley town centre is quite compact, and upon exit from the station make your way across the forecourt to walk up Foundry Hill, right adjacent the eponymous café bar, which is recommended as a coda to the walk. Cross the main road to the theatre opposite and, before bearing half left towards Myrtle Park in front of Bingley Pool, you might inspect the ancient (although twice re-sited) Market Stance and Butter Cross to the right-hand side of the theatre; a reminder that Bingley has a long history. Keep on the diagonal trajectory across little Myrtle Park passing close to the bandstand

(coffees and other refreshaments are available in the café by the bowling green) and cross the River Aire on the footbridge. Walk up past the allotments and turn right at the end, bringing you back down to another bridge, by a ford and a very handsome old yeoman's house in the local gritstone, complete with mullions and all the trimmings. The path leads over the bridge and via a couple of stiles onto another wide track, but only as far as a signed path that leads off to the left by another house, then directly out onto a golf course. Follow the white stone markers as directed and keep a sharp lookout for golf balls before the right of way reaches the foot of the tree-clad hillside ahead. The large mansion close by is Harden

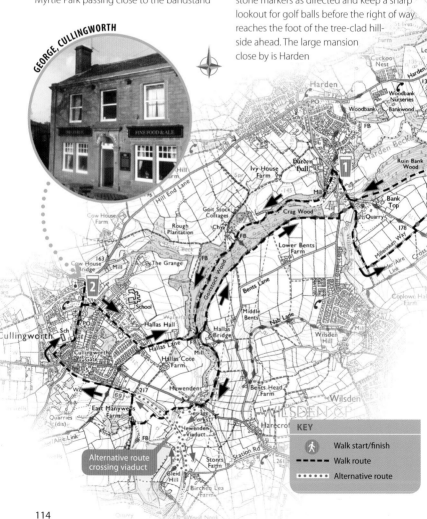

GEORGE, CULLINGWORTH

KEY

Walk start/finish

- - - Walk route

····· Alternative route

Alternative route crossing viaduct

114

IN THE FOUNDRY HILL, BINGLEY

a little to the right; now just keep on the wide track ignoring side-shoots. You'll reach a folly, known as St David's ruins. The owner of Harden Grange, Benjamin Ferrand, built this as a romantic ruin in 1796, in accordance with the gothic fashion of the time.

It's now plain sailing, and the track brings you downhill again before disgorging you first onto an unadopted road (bear right) and, straight after, onto a rather busy road. Irritatingly the 200-yard section between here and the riverside pub ahead, which is our first call, has no footpath, so the usual rules apply: single file, walk on the right, facing the traffic. Make sure drivers can see you: a partially opened-out map or similar is helpful. With good fortune arrive unscathed at the 🍺 **Malt** in a couple of minutes. This pub has recently been modernised and had its name truncated; the interior still has some charcter but visually the exterior is more appealing. You'll be more interested in the beers, which are from Theakstons with one from Caledonian; and this pub with its attractive garden and patio area is well-sited as a halfway refreshment stop on the outward leg of this walk.

Grange, acquired by the Ferrand family of Tory politicians in the 17th century. Shortly there is a very steep section on a widened track that has had the recent attention of heavy plant at the time of writing, before the track levels off again and veers around

The Folly, Harden

The next stage of the walk keeps far closer to Harden Beck as we enter Goitstock Wood, a local beauty spot. Cross the river bridge by the pub and bear hard left into Goitstock Lane. The first half a mile or so leads along a minor lane adjacent the stream, and, perhaps unsurprisingly, 'Harden & Bingley Park' turns out to be a caravan park. Follow the roadway through it (mercifully brief) but look out for the former chimney, across the river to the right, of the old Goit Stock cotton mill. Improbable as it seems, in the 1920s Goit Stock was a thriving pleasure resort, the mill having been converted to a ballroom and café and drawing a record crowd of 20,000 on a bank holiday Monday in 1927! But tragedy struck that same evening when the old mill went up in flames, destroying both the famous dance floor and the instruments of the Wilsden Brass Band; and that was that.

Malt, Harden

The scenery improves dramatically now, and in the right weather the woodland path close to the stream is idylllic and generally easy to navigate. The best bit of scenery in the wood is probably Goit Stock falls, beyond which is a footbridge where paths converge. Our route continues upstream: bear sharp left for a few yards before resuming your previous trajectory at the signpost for 'Hewenden'. Pass alongside the former Hallas Bridge Mill (now converted to residential use), the path now climbing more steadily, and soon the dramatic Hewenden Viaduct comes into view (see box). Drop down to the road (and again take care here), but before you reach it it's as well to consult the map and decide if you want to cross the viaduct on foot or take the slightly shorter direct route. If the former, take the second, riverside path signed on the left having turned downhill on the road. If the latter, walk on, crossing the stream, and take the next path. Note that in either case direct access to the viaduct is not possible and both routes involve some detour to reach a level access to the Trail because the embankment leading to the viaduct is higher than the approach paths that pass under it. I recommend doubling back to enable you to cross the viaduct as views from it are well worth the detour.

HEWENDEN VIADUCT AND THE GREAT NORTHERN RAILWAY

The Great Northern Railway in 1870 had reached Halifax and Bradford and was looking to push north towards Keighley. The topography was adverse, but this was never something to deter Victorian railway engineers. The line necessitated a couple of long tunnels, the 1000-yard Strines cutting at Queensbury, and several viaducts. That across the Hewenden valley has 17 arches, each up to 37 m (123 ft) high and spanning 15 m (50 ft), making it one of the loftiest in the country. Moreover, it was necessary to dig the foundations almost to the same depth as the height in order to find stability in sandy soil. The stone viaduct has a gentle curve and was one of the scenic highlights of the line. It is now part of the Sustrans Great Northern Railway Trail for cyclists and walkers.

Walking north into the outskirts of Cullingworth, you're on one of the few accessible stretches of the old trackbed which the charity Sustrans hope to extend as part of the Great Northern Railway Trail. In fact, just after crossing the Cullingworth Viaduct – a notable feature in its own right – the trail ends and you have to bear off to the right. Head down to the main road, and turning left it's about a five-minute walk down the street before you reach Church Street on the left with a full-on view of the striking St John's church. More importantly, only coming into view when you turn 20 yards down towards the church is the **2 George**, occupying a prominent position on the square. The George is one of those pubs rescued from mediocrity by enterprising new licencees and which is now a destination for both food and drink. The building itself has an appealing interior, with some opening out of former rooms around a central servery but still plenty of intimate corners. Décor and furnishings are well chosen, and a fine terrazzo floor survives. From our perspective the highlight is a wide range of locally brewed beers from the nearby Old Spot brewery, good enough to have won

Goit Stock Falls

the pub CAMRA awards and establish it as a regular in the *Good Beer Guide*. It's a comfortable sort of place that you might be tempted to linger in, washing down lunch with a couple more beers; in the event of which it's reassuring to know you've just walked past the bus stop from where, if need be, you can return to the likes of nearby Keighley or Haworth. It's also possible to continue the walk as a linear route to Haworth (closer than you think: consult your OS map) to link with Walk 12.

For walkers returning to Bingley by the 'official' route, return to the war memorial on the main road and make for the Co-op store on the far side of it (on Greenside Lane), turning right beyond it onto a road of nondescript houses and bungalows that climbs gently uphill.

At the top, turn left onto the Hallas Lane, an old trackway that leads out of the built-up area of Cullingworth and (ignoring paths to right and left) down to the footbridge you encountered earlier, by the old Hallas Bridge Mill. Head up the brae on the right bank once more but this time continue ahead towards the terrace of old cottages, bearing left in front of the first row (very

The ford, Bingley

indistinct signage) and, at the end, over to and through a stile, which gives onto a clear path running along the top of Goitstock Wood.

The Market Stance and Butter Cross, Bingley

Now the simple instructions are: continue on this path for over a mile passing under two sets of overhead pylons in quick succession. Although on the map you're very close to the outward route, which is down in the valley steeply below you, the scenery is quite different. The lane you eventually reach is the same one I berated earlier for its lack of a footpath. Once again it's a short stretch along this surprisingly busy road (turning left from the path) and again the same complaint is valid so take care, although the signed path heading off to the right is visible straightaway. The path takes you down to cross a small beck and then back up to a gate onto a wider track winding uphill. Follow this up for 100 yards as it curves right, but then leave it as it starts to veer left, onto a signed path heading south, above but parallel to the stream in its little valley. This path should be followed until, in a few minutes, it leads steadily left via a memorial plaque on a large boulder to the top wall, where an earthen path leads right and left. Looking right you should see a stile and another path then bearing left across fields, and this is our route, which in turn reaches a minor road in a further five minutes' walking.

Now, once again, the clearly signed way ahead is almost opposite; and it's quite easy to follow the worn trod in the grass when it soon veers left towards the woods, the same belt of conifers encountered early in the walk. Enter the woods and very quickly meet up with the wide path at the top of the steep incline, which you will doubtless recall. Now it's an easy matter to retrace your steps into Bingley across the golf course; don't forget to turn left by the allotments!

In Bingley you'll be in need of top-up refreshment after the four-mile hike since the George. I recommend you make for the **3 Foundry Hill** opposite the station forecourt and down the short eponymous street directly facing the theatre. A very modern bar of which Bingley has a number, this one takes its beer very seriously and you can expect to choose between five changing cask ales. Moreover, food is served pretty much all day until mid evening so, given its location, it's a good spot to end up in especially if you eventually require a train.

For more possibilities in Bingley either consult your *Good Beer Guide* or try the recently reborn and renamed **4 Potting Shed**, previously the Fleece, which you'll find five minutes' walk away on the main road (heading north) and which offers 4 cask ales and homemade pizzas. If this is too modern for you, Timothy Taylor's Brown Cow is just beyond, across Ireland Bridge over the Aire.

PUB INFORMATION

1 MALT
Wilsden Road, Harden, BD16 1BG
01535 272357
www.themaltharden.co.uk
Opening hours: 12-11 (10.30 Sun)

2 GEORGE
Station Road, Cullingworth, BD13 5HN
01535 275566 • thegeorgecullingworth.co.uk
Opening hours: 12-11 (midnight Fri & Sat)

3 FOUNDRY HILL
Wellington Street, Bingley, BD16 2NB
01274 566144 • foundryhillbar.co.uk
Opening hours: closed Mon & Tue; 12-midnight (11 Wed); 12-9 Sun

Try also:

4 POTTING SHED
94 Main Street, Bingley, BD16 2JH
01274 512635 • www.thepottingshedbingley.co.uk
Opening hours: 12-11 (midnight Thu; 1am Fri & Sat)

Saltaire, Shipley Glen & Baildon

WALK 18

An excellent round combining interesting canalside walking with the ascent of Baildon Moor rising to over 900 feet with views to match. Linking them is attractive Shipley Glen, which has the feel of a far more remote spot than it really is. As a reward for the bracing ascent, there is the usual galaxy of fine pubs to choose from, and, if the weather suits, you could finish a lazy riverside afternoon in the Boathouse having enjoyed the cultural appeal of Titus Salt's industrial model village at Saltaire, now inscribed on the list of World Heritage sites.

▸ **Start/finish:** Saltaire railway station

▸ **Access:** 15 mins from Leeds or Bradford by rail

▸ **Distance:** 6.5 miles (10.5 km)

▸ **OS map:** Explorer 288

▸ **Key attractions:** Saltaire World Heritage Site; Shipley Glen & Tramway; Leeds–Liverpool canal

▸ **THE PUBS:** Bull's Head Inn, Junction, both Baildon; Fanny's Ale & Cider House, Boathouse Inn, both Saltaire. Try also: Ring o' Bells, Shipley

▸ **Timing tip:** Lunch service at the Junction ends at 2pm, so planning to arrive at the first pub shortly after midday is a good idea.

Saltaire's United Reformed Church

On the canal at Saltaire

Saltaire station is located centrally in the heart of the World Heritage site opposite Titus Salt's mill, now a shopping experience of sorts, and adjacent to the grid of streets he laid out in 1850, endowed with solidly attractive homes for his workers (see box). When you alight from the train, walk up to the mill and then turn left down the wide street, passing his handsome United Reformed Church with its distinctive conical tower, and thence to the canal, these days of course a leisure artery. Cross the canal and then make for the river footbridge just beyond, noting the enviable location of the Boathouse right on the Aire, and a destination for later should you still have the stamina.

Over the bridge brings you directly into Roberts Park; follow the perimeter wall of the park up to the northernmost point. Leave the park by the gates, making directly across the leisure centre car park to the entrance to Shipley Glen

Tramway which you probably noticed through the park railings minutes earlier. If it's open, you can save your legs and for £1 take the short ride to the top, otherwise it's a short climb on the path through the woods alongside the track.

At the top follow unexciting Plod Lane for a few minutes to reach the Glen House pub and tea rooms, and immediately beyond turn left into an open landscape with a wide bridleway making its way through trees into

On Baildon Bank

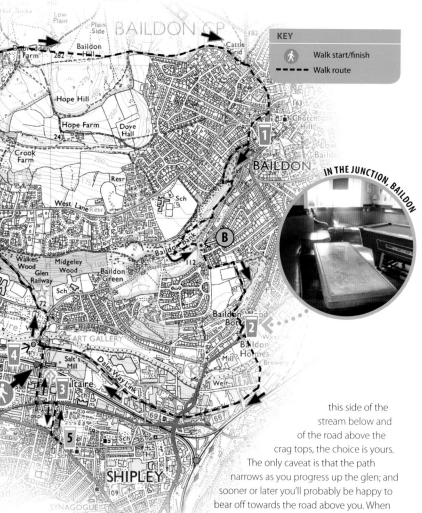

IN THE JUNCTION, BAILDON

this side of the
stream below and
of the road above the
crag tops, the choice is yours.
The only caveat is that the path
narrows as you progress up the glen; and
sooner or later you'll probably be happy to
bear off towards the road above you. When
you do and reach the road verge, look for a
point where the wall following the far side
of the road turns away at 90 degrees by a
double path sign.

Here (**A** 🕐 130398), take the wide
bridleway, which makes for the left-hand end
of a line of trees on the horizon. It's a steady
uphill plod for 10 minutes or so, and, yes, it is
an incongrously sited not-so-mobile home
park that you're approaching. Navigation
round it is easy, though: follow the wall
round and, as it veers away to the right by
the farm buildings, simply continue on the
obvious track uphill towards the highest

Shipley Glen. Almost at once the
town feels a long way behind;
follow the main track that runs gently downhill through mature deciduous woodland,
and at a scissor crossing of paths bear right,
more or less following the contour. Stroll
between a reservoir visible through the
trees below you and the sandstone outcrops
marking the escarpment above you on your
right. Shipley Glen is a deservedly popular
spot, although, if you have made a prompt
start, you should not have too many others
following you. Several paths branch off to
left and right: basically, as long as you stay

SALTAIRE

Saltaire was developed around 1850 by the Victorian industrialist Titus Salt when he moved his milling interests from Bradford to an open site at the edge of Shipley. At the time it was the largest of many model communities built by industrial philanthropists for their workers. Houses were well built and appointed, and Salt ensured that an abundance of social and community facilities for the physical and spiritual well-being of his workforce were provided. As such, Saltaire is regarded as an important development in the history of 19th-century urban planning. Sir Titus died in 1876 and was interred in the mausoleum adjacent to the striking Congregational (now the

United Reformed) church. The town, which has survived remarkably intact, was inscribed on the UNSECO list of World Heritage sites in 2001, and the whole place is a Conservation Area. The mill itself closed in 1986 but has been restored and now houses a mixture of business, commerce, leisure and residential uses.

To continue, head off in broadly the same easterly direction, again on a good path, which you can see as it continues below you alongside the edge of a housing estate in Baildon. Just before you reach the road, fork right at a scissor junction of paths, still keeping close to the back fences of residences, and with the church tower directly ahead of you, to emerge by the golf clubhouse and thence to the main road running downhill into Baildon, about a five-minute walk. Despite some nondescript suburbs, the centre of old Baildon is still a pleasant place with some reminders of its past as an industrial town. At the roundabout a short distance past the Malt Shovel pub, bear right into Westgate and almost immediately you reach the

1 Bull's Head Inn. This simple but modernised two-roomed pub is mainly a community local, but a friendly one at that and one that serves a good range of well-kept ales – Saltaire Blonde is one of the regulars, and the pub offers up to three changing guest beers.

When you leave the Bull's Head, continue along Westgate bearing left into Bank View and left again, whereupon at the end of this street take the right-hand (first) of two signed paths; this one will shortly carry you along the top of Baildon Bank, offering great vistas from an unexpectedly steep and lofty perch. The distant and prominent chimney is that of the famous Lister's Mill in Bradford, which looks unexpectedly close from here.

Take the flight of steps steeply down past some benches, and bearing off right onto an earthen path reach a plateau of sorts halfway down the bank, and continue, following the course of a good track. Soon, more or less when a second flight of concrete steps peels off uphill, you see below you a road running away at right angles alongside parkland; we want to take this road, but the easiest way to

point of the skyline, which is soon reached, by the white Triangulation pillar. (For the benefit of younger readers these familiar 'Trig points' were formerly used for mapping and are frequently sited on hilltops and viewpoints). Here the height is 282 metres, over 900 feet. A circular orientation table will help you enjoy the view, weather permitting.

Junction, Baildon

get down to it without a very steep descent is to continue on the path, for a few more minutes, until another path doubles back sharply left at an acute angle. Following this will enable you to reach the road junction (by the bus shelter) and walk away up Cliffe Lane West (**B** 📍 150388). But not for long – at the end of the houses on your left bear left along a wide track alongside the football pitch, and then right to keep the pitch alongside you (over a wall) past a phone mast. Follow the path round to the right yet again and join a road, Baildon Wood Court. Here, bear left at the first opportunity and take two successive, short, signed footpaths, the first at the foot of the brae here and then again downhill to emerge on the main Baildon Road almost opposite the **2 Junction**.

A real landmark by virtue both of its prominent position and

of its bulk, this is a handsome traditional pub, which has earned a good reputation for its extensive beer range mixing some regulars, including Saltaire Blonde again and, unusually, Fullers ESB, with changing guests from all over. Beers from the in-house Junction Brewery often feature. It's got a lot to offer as a building, too, having retained three distinct drinking rooms and avoided over-heavy modernisation. My favourite is the room in the apex, where there is some fine fitted bench seating. A limited but quite adequate lunchtime menu is served until 2pm.

Navigation back into Saltaire is a breeze: come out of the pub and bear hard left along the pub wall on the busy Otley Road, and at the end of it you'll be opposite a residential street running downhill to the River Aire. Carefully cross (at the lights if necessary) and take this over the river and onward for another two minutes to reach the canal.

Fanny's, Saltaire

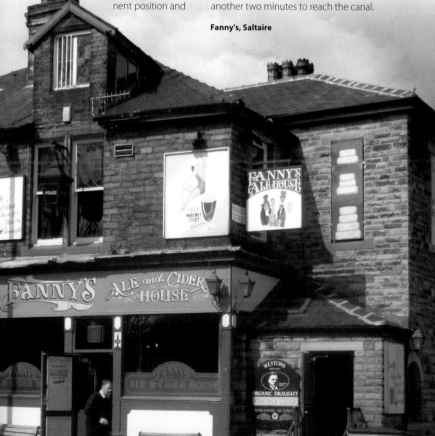

The bar inside Fanny's Ale & Cider House

Turning right onto the towpath (signed the Aire Valley Greenway), follow it (not without interest) right back to the bridge in the centre of Saltaire which you crossed at the outset. There is little to be gained by the alternative of leaving at bridge 207 and walking into the Salts Mill complex, but during daytime hours this is possible and will eventually allow you to regain Victoria Road pretty much opposite the railway station. Either way, head up Victoria Road to the first main road junction and, bearing left, it's no more than a couple of minutes' walk along to **Fanny's Ale & Cider House**.

This welcoming pub, formerly a beer shop, is now a free house and stocks three regular ales, up to five guests and a craft keg beer, as well as draught ciders. An extension has increased seating capacity downstairs and added disabled access. Upstairs there is a room with comfortable seating. The gas-lit lounge is adorned with breweriana, and in winter real fires make it a cosy hangout.

At this point it's an option to take in the *Good Beer Guide*-listed Ring o'Bells, which, although listed as in nearby Shipley, is little more than five minutes' walk away. Cross the road (carefully: it's very busy) opposite Fanny's and walk uphill on Park Street to the A650 at the top, and, bearing left, you will immediately see the **5** **Ring o' Bells** on the road fork. It's a substantial and not unattractive roadhouse in solid Yorkshire

stone; inside it has been opened out with the exception of one room. Beers are well kept: expect to find Leeds Pale, a couple from Timothy Taylor's nearby Keighley brewery, and some guests. Return to Fanny's by the same route when you're done; and from there make your way down towards the station by further retracing your steps; and thence to your final calling point, the **Boathouse**.

The light and modern café-style interior may or may not be to your taste, but if the weather is fine it hardly matters as you can sit on the riverside terrace and watch the world go by whilst enjoying a good choice of cask ales: Black Sheep Bitter and the almost ubiquitous Saltaire Blonde, joined by up to four guests. The rather premium prices perhaps reflect the attractive waterside setting; and it's but a very short step back to the station.

PUB INFORMATION

1 **BULL'S HEAD INN**
6 Westgate, Baildon, BD17 5ES
01274 976416
Opening hours: 12-11.30 (midnight Fri & Sat)

2 **JUNCTION**
1 Baildon Road, Baildon, BD17 6AB
01274 582009
Opening hours: 12-midnight (1am Fri & Sat)

3 **FANNY'S ALE & CIDER HOUSE**
63 Saltaire Road, Saltaire, BD18 3JN
01274 591419
Opening hours: 12 (5 Mon)-11; 12-midnight Fri & Sat

4 **BOATHOUSE INN**
Victoria Road, Saltaire, BD18 3LA
01274 585690 • www.theboathouseinn.co.uk
Opening hours: 12-10.30 (11.30 Fri-Sun)

Try also:

5 **RING O' BELLS**
3 Bradford Road, Shipley, BD18 3PR
01274 584386
Opening hours: 11-midnight (1am Fri & Sat); 12-11 Sun

Over the Chevin to Otley

WALK

19

Reputedly described by J.M.W. Turner as the finest viewpoint under 1,000 feet in England, the Otley Chevin is the highlight of the walk. The great artist often stayed at nearby Farnley Hall, and the extensive views from the top of the Chevin across Wharfedale were one of his favourite subjects. Gentle on the southern side but steep on the north, well-wooded slopes conceal a network of paths and a nicely sited café. Otley itself is a pleasant old town with several noteworthy buildings and a large weekend market. The town centre is extremely well pubbed, making the temptation to linger a strong one; and if you really can't face the steep pull out of town and back over the shoulder of the Chevin, frequent buses are on hand to take you back either to the railway at Menston or into Guiseley, where further refreshment is available before heading back to the station.

> **Start/finish:** Guiseley railway station

> **Access:** Trains from Leeds, Skipton or Bradford

> **Distance:** 7 miles (11 km) for circuit; 4.7 miles to Otley

> **OS map:** Explorer 297

> **Key attractions:** Chevin Forest Park; Otley – historic market town (market Friday & Saturday), Old Grammar School Gallery, Wharfe Meadows Park

> **THE PUBS:** Royalty, Junction Inn, Old Cock, Horse & Farrier, all Otley; Factory Workers' Club, Guiseley. Try also: Fleece, Otley; Coopers, Guiseley

> **Timing tips:** Save this walk for a pleasant day since the ridge of the Chevin is exposed to the weather; and why not aim for Friday or Saturday to catch the buzz at Otley market? The Royalty, about 2.5 miles into the walk, opens at 12 noon

Otley from the Chevin

FLEECE, OTLEY

THE FLEECE

JUNCTION INN, OTLEY

THE JUNCTION INN

KEY

🚶 Walk start/finish

- - - - Walk route

From either the railway station at Guiseley or the bus stop (alight at the supermarket on the main Otley Road), it's a very short step to the road junction with Oxford Road, leading east towards a mini roundabout (5–7 minutes' walk) with a stone cross and the old village stocks. Be sure to take the correct road here: to the right you can see the tower of the parish church of St Oswald, whereas left on Town Street the Guiseley Factory Workers' Club (possible later stop) lies a short distance up the hill. The route you want is Queensway, the road running straight ahead across the roundabout.

In about 150 yards, leave the road on a signed footpath to the left. Cross a farm track after about 500 yards (slightly left, then right, but signed), and then begins a generally gentle walk up towards the Chevin, which from this angle is barely noticeable as a landscape feature. Keep to the right of the next field close to the small stream, and thereafter the route, although it winds around, is very well defined. Where you meet a choice of routes

Old Cock, Otley

after a mile or so, ignore the left fork and continue straight ahead. Shortly after passing an abandoned treehouse, at another path junction, take the right-hand option towards the farmhouse ahead.

Now, at the farmstead ignore the signed path pointing to the right, and instead walk up the farm road between buildings to meet a public road very shortly. Here the way ahead – Mall Lane – is almost opposite and aims directly for the horizon, steepening somewhat as you pass another farmstead and enter an enclosed bridleway that runs

uphill. It's still fairly easy going, however, and it will come as a surprise when, before long, you see how high you've climbed. At the top road take the wide unmade track almost opposite, and in no time you reach the very top of the whaleback ridge of the Chevin by a gate into the Chevin Forest Park. The corresponding view half a mile away at the car park is called 'Surprise View', but that applies at least as much here, for you're looking out across Wharfedale at the scene that inspired Turner. Your eye may be drawn to a curious tor-like outcrop to the

Descent from the Chevin into Otley

Stepped path on the Chevin

north-east: this is Almscliff Crag, a complex gritstone mass popular with climbers, whose form owes something to a subsea landslip far back in geological history.

The route now leads into the Forest Park through the gate and along the wide, well-walked track along the summit ridge. In no time the orientaion table by the car park is reached, not quite the highest point but with very fine views to Otley below and well beyond. (Each Easter a huge cross-like beacon adorns this part of the ridge.) The prominent white building to your left on the road is a thoughtfully sited reward for your efforts in getting here, so I recommend making your way through the car park and carefully across the road to the recently revamped **1 Royalty**. This roadhouse makes a welcome stop before heading downhill into Otley. Two changing cask beers are available, and simple lunchtime food – a variety of sandwiches and jacket potatoes – is obtainable until 3pm.

Return through the car park to the Chevin path. It's possible to head directly downhill from here, but I recommend a rather less brutal alternative: retrace your earlier steps 50 yards east and take the flagged

path diagonally downhill, then in a further 100 yards double back sharply on an earthen track leading downhill into the trees. Keep on the same trajectory, itself fairly steep, and you'll eventually see the stepped path from the top of the hill joining from the left. Just beyond here is the White House, which is open until 2pm for light refreshments Monday to Friday (3pm weekends; closed Tuesdays). It's run by adults with learning difficulties, supported by Leeds City Council. Continue either down the stepped, steep path straight downhill or take the gentler alternative heading out west of the White House yard (orange waymark) and curving round to the right to rejoin the direct route by a tarmac track and metal gate at the foot of the steps (**A** 204446). Now take the footpath opposite, passing Elvies Wood down to join Birdcage Walk. Directly opposite here is a footbridge across the new bypass (built along the line of the former railway), which leads straight into town via Station Road.

The centre of Otley is pleasant and compact, focused upon the Market Square. Just before reaching it, Bondgate bears off to the right. Along on the north side, at the junction with Charles Street, is the **2 Junction Inn**. If you like solid traditional pubs, this handsome gritstone corner house is for you: and, once inside, it has a welcoming feel with several distinct areas radiating off a central fireplace. The licensee is rightly proud of his Timothy Taylor's Landlord; but there's plenty of choice besides, with several guest beers alongside the Taylor's and Theakston's regulars. A real cider and a wide range of malt whiskies are in the supporting cast. A collection of leather harnesses and saddles, plus pictures of old Otley and numerous metal beer adverts and mirrors, contribute to the atmosphere.

Now retracing your steps, turn right into Crossgate, and before you reach the little bus station you'll arrive at the **3 Old Cock** on the right. Another traditional two-roomed pub in a solid old stone building, you might think. However, it was converted from a café as recently as 2010, which accounts for the third, upstairs room. Downstairs it feels as if it's been here for centuries. A large range of excellent, mostly locally brewed beers, is served, which has won the Old Cock a string of local CAMRA awards in its short life as a pub. At least two real ciders are also available, plus a range of foreign beers.

If you want to eat more than crisps and nuts in Otley, then you'll need to look further than the first two otherwise excellent pubs: from the Old Cock walk down past the bus station and turn left into Boroughgate, which leads to the Market Place. If you find the characterful frontage of the Bay Horse on the north side of the market, there's a small alleyway ('ginnel' in these parts), Bay Horse Court, immediately to the left. Take this short cut through to Bridge Street and you'll see the **4 Horse & Farrier** to your right. Here is an open-plan, café-bar-style pub housed in a traditional building. Even the beer garden is in a modern style, more like a patio. The pub has plenty of food,

Bay Horse, Otley

rooms (if you want to base yourself in Otley) and, happily, eight handpumps offering another wide range of beers. Taylor and Rooster breweries usually feature, otherwise you could find anything. There's a decent selection of bottled foreign beers, too.

Whilst here, decide on the course of action for when you leave. There are recommended pubs in Guiseley, but, if you wish to try another in Otley first, see my recommendation below. If you are walking back, remember the steep hill. Otherwise, buses leave from the bus station: the 33/33A and 967 among others serve Menston (the nearest rail station) and Guiseley itself. Walking out of town, follow Bridge Street back (either through the ginnel again and via the Market Place) or continue round on the road to the Black Horse, a splendid-looking old coaching inn with its old stables on a corner of the market, and turn right into Westgate. Follow Westgate for several minutes as far as the traditional-looking **6 Fleece**, which is an excellent choice for another beer stop, on

Horse & Farrier, Otley

account of the eight handpumps serving a great range of beers including several from the local Wharfe Bank brewery. Talking of the Wharfe, on a fine day the super beer garden here, which runs right down to the river, is a great place to linger, by which time you may well be walking back for that bus…

But, if you're heading back over the Chevin, there's more road walking to do first, starting with forking left by the Fleece on Piper Lane, and then taking West Chevin Road on the left in some 250 yards. Now continue over the bypass, following the road as it winds to the right and heads uphill. Look out for a footpath sign in a further 300 yards, and gird your loins for a steep and steady uphill plod into the trees. The gradient eases a little where the main ridge path is met; but there's still a little way more to climb. Cross to the path heading slightly left uphill, and follow this until you see a stile in the top wall appearing through the trees on the right. Alternatively, follow a less distinct track through the trees close to the wall, and follow it at a 90-degree left turn to reach the same stile (**B** 🌐 195442).

Guiseley stocks

Now things are easy: walk across the field to the road and cross over following the signed path. You're now heading south and, aside from a short detour to the left to avoid some workings by the buildings ahead, you stay on a southward trajectory right down towards Guiseley. Merge with the road at the bottom of the farm lane and then it's straight down into town until, yards before the junction with the stocks and cross, you see the **5** **Factory Workers' Club** on the left. This friendly club was founded over 100 years ago by the Yeadon and Guiseley Factory Workers' Union. It serves three changing guest ales from micros and independents from anywhere in the UK, usually including a dark beer. A popular beer festival is held every April. CAMRA members are welcome with this guide or a membership card.

Finally, the walk back to the station means retracing your steps along Oxford Road from the mini roundabout; but those with stamina might want to try **7** **Coopers** on the Otley Road which, inside a rather bland exterior, serves up to eight interesting and changing ales in a modern café bar/brasserie atmosphere, as well as offering food. Ask for directions from the factory club.

PUB INFORMATION

1 ROYALTY
Yorkgate, Otley, LS21 3DG
01943 463735 • www.the-royalty.co.uk
Opening hours: 12-11

2 JUNCTION INN
44 Bondgate, Otley, LS21 1AD
01943 463233
Opening hours: 11 (11.30 Thu)-11; 11-midnight Fri & Sat; 12-10.30 Sun

3 OLD COCK
11-13 Crossgate, Otley, LS21 1AA
01943 464424 • theoldcockotley.co.uk
Opening hours: 11-11

4 HORSE & FARRIER
7 Bridge Street, Otley, LS21 1BQ
01943 468400
Opening hours: 12-11

5 FACTORY WORKERS' CLUB
6 Town Street, Guiseley, LS20 9DT
01943 874793 • www.guiseleyfactoryworkersclub.co.uk
Opening hours: 1-11 (midnight Fri); 11.30-midnight Sat; 11-11 Sun

Try also:

6 FLEECE
Westgate, Otley, LS21 3DT
01943 465034
Opening hours: 12-midnight

7 COOPERS
4-6 Otley Road, Guiseley, LS20 8AH
01943 878835
Opening hours: 12-11 (midnight Fri & Sat)

Wortley & the Upper Don Valley

WALK 20

Wortley packs quite a punch for small place. Formerly part of a rural industrial area with metalworking and quarrying prominent, the attractive village boasts a splendid hall (now dubbed the 'Workers' Stately Home') and gardens, several handsome buildings, a thriving village shop and café, the Wortley Arms and, to cap it all, the nearby Wortley Men's Club, which won CAMRA's 2015 award for Club of the Year. Take a CAMRA membership card or a copy of this guide to get in. Coupled with several worthwhile sights *en route*, it's worth making a day of this round; and, if you're able to do this walk on a Sunday or bank holiday, you'll be able to enjoy a visit to the Wortley Top Forge museum, which is otherwise closed.

▶ **Start/finish:** Wortley village, adjacent parish church

▶ **Access:** Bus 29 links with rail stations at Sheffield, Penistone and Chapeltown

▶ **Distance:** 5.7 miles (9.2 km)

▶ **OS map:** Explorer 278

▶ **Key attractions:** Wortley Hall (www.wortleyhall.org.uk); Wortley Top Forge museum (www.topforge.co.uk); industrial archaeology at Hunshelf; Huthwaite Hall; Trans Pennine Trail (www.transpenninetrail.org.uk)

▶ **THE PUBS:** Bridge Inn, Thurgoland; Wortley Arms, Wortley Men's Club, both Wortley

▶ **Timing tip:** The Bridge Inn is now shut until 4pm on Mondays

Heather and gorse abound on the route

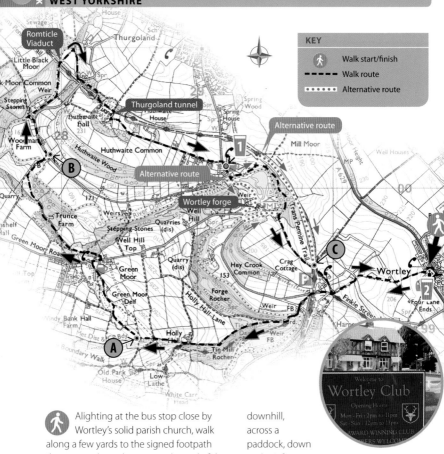

Alighting at the bus stop close by Wortley's solid parish church, walk along a few yards to the signed footpath that passes through a gate at the end of the churchyard. Even at the outset the view over the valley of the Don is extensive. It's a pity to lose height straight away, but that is exactly what happens, albeit without the problems of route finding; since the path right down to the valley floor below is on a pedestrian highway of large rectangular stone blocks laid very neatly against each other. It makes for a speedy descent to the foot of the slope, where you join the road opposite the gardens of the old railway station, now long defunct but once a busy railhead for the industrial products of the area, notably the stone from quarries that were worked locally.

Take the road under the rail bridge and then, at the T-junction, look for a footpath sign across the road and slightly left, bisecting the two roads. This leads you downhill, across a paddock, down to the infant River Don, well hidden in the trees. This is the old Wortley Leppings (or 'leapings'). Note the attractive old mill to the left, and the submerged stone setts of the old ford. Choose the bridge or the stepping stones to cross and bear right, passing a couple of old stone gateposts before bearing left uphill on a wide earthen track. Just 50 yards up, by a waymarked crossing of paths, bear right again on a wide track, which climbs again into the woods, quite steeply.

After some 150 yards the track reaches three stone gateposts. At this point take the left fork, up through the rhododendron bushes. You're now ascending the ridge leading to Hunshelf Bank, more obvious in winter when the trees have shed their leaves. This is the time you're more likely to be able to see, through the trees and down to your left, the Tin Mill Dam – a reservoir now used as a fishery, but once connected with the eponymous 18th-century works – for this area was noted for metalworking as well as stone quarrying. Industrial archaeology geeks may enjoy the download about the tin mill and other local sites on the East Peak Industrial Heritage website (industrial-heritage.epip.org.uk).

The gradient levels off and, whilst a wall and field beyond appear on the right, the scene to your left is of a precipitous drop down the bank to the river valley and the fast bypass road with Stocksbridge beyond.

Continue until the path exits onto the roadway in front of Holly Hall. Here bear left and continue through a gate before bearing right, uphill again, on the obvious track towards the wind turbine ahead. Keep the turbine on your left and bear right a little to cross a ramshackle stile, passing under the electricity cables; and now keep straight on with the stone wall on your right and the drop into the valley below immediately on your left. This grassy path through the bracken offers great views across to Stocksbridge, whose steelworks continue the long history of metalworking locally. If you have brought a flask and/or other refreshments, and if the weather is favourable, it's a great spot to enjoy a rest and the panorama.

Descent through the woods at Green Moor

Where the wall dog-legs a few yards to the left (Ⓐ 🧭 286989), very shortly after you pass under the electric cables, go through the gate and head across the field on the indistinct path towards the copse opposite, crossing a stile to enter it. The steps down encountered immediately (which can be slippery so need care in the damp) mark the edge of the former Delph Quarry. Now abandoned and overgrown, this was one of the first large quarries in the region worked for stone roofing slates and fine-grained green stone, used widely by the Victorians. Keep right (ignore the path left going up

Wortley Hall

some steps), and just beyond here at a junction bear left, walking down through the Delph to join the road in Green Moor by a red phone box, which is used as an information point. Green Moor is an old industrial village once pitted with quarries, in addition to the Delph, which you've just walked through. An informative display board adjacent the phone box tells part of the story; and across the road are the village stocks, which were re-erected here to commemorate the coronation of King George VI in 1937.

Cross over to the stocks and bear right along the road for about 100 yards; then take a footpath alongside a bungalow, leading through a gate and over a step stile into a wooded dell, as you descend rapidly from the summit ridge. Bear left along a wire fence, and keep straight ahead at the next junction, noting fine views through the trees. Over a stile by a metal gate, continue downhill past Trunch Farm on a pleasant wide farm track. In the trees on the left is the site of California, the last of Green Moor's quarries to be filled in, and probably so named as it was opened at the time that the frontier movement reached the US west coast. The path steepens towards the valley

Romticle Viaduct is now part of the Trans Pennine Trail

floor as you follow the track round to the right across a meadow and, crossing the river on a footbridge, walk up to join the very quiet lane at (**B** 🕐 279002). Turn left and stroll along the lane.

At Don House, where the lane bears right, disregard the footpath sign here unless you want to detour 100 yards down to visit the stepping stones over the river. The path you want leads off in a further 100 yards, where the road bears right again. It passes a heavily (probably too heavily) restored old mill and manicured gardens. Take the left fork to keep to the riverbank just beyond, and walk towards the striking Romticle Viaduct ahead. Now part of the Sustrans Trans-Pennine Trail, the line was part of the former Woodhead Railway engineered by Joseph Locke which opened in 1845 and operated until 1981. Pass under the viaduct and walk across to the stile. Here the more obvious path continues to the left up a wooded bank. Disregard this, and instead turn right to follow the wall on a path that can be a little overgrown in summer, but nonetheless leads shortly up a bank and brings you out onto the old track bed, in view of the Thurgoland tunnel. However, as you bear left onto the Trans-Pennine Trail, head immediately up a slope to the left again, ascending to a bridge over the track bed; but keep straight ahead on a clear path that climbs right above the tunnel entrance: you can see the trackbed beneath you through the trees.

Continue south, more or less above the line of the tunnel below, emerging into a paddock containing, to your right, the outbuildings of Huthwaite Hall. The right of way leads down towards the Hall, and across the paddock in front of it giving you a fine view of the handsome elevation of this well-proportioned Georgian house, dating to 1748 and built by John Carr for John Cockshutt, owner of Wortley ironworks.

The Leppings, an ancient crossing point

Once onto the carriage drive of the Hall, it's a straight and simple linear walk down towards the main road in about half a mile; on the way you pass Huthwaite House on the left, in itself a pretty impressive building. Turn right at the road and a few yards sees you in the car park of the 🍺 **Bridge Inn**.

The Bridge is a smartened-up traditional two-roomed pub, though the left-hand room is now a dining area. Inside the pleasant bar is a log-burning stove, and there's a small snug-alcove in the far corner. At present it offers a couple of beers from nearby Wentworth brewery and a rotating guest from elsewhere. It's also an obvious place to eat, with food served all day until 8pm (5pm on Sundays). A pleasant grassy beer garden is sited beyond the car park.

Whilst you're in the Bridge Inn, it's worth studying the map for your onward options. All routes rejoin at the bridge over the old railway at (**C** 🕓 298994), but if it's a Sunday or a bank holiday I'd recommended taking in Wortley Top Forge nearby. It's the oldest surviving water-powered iron forge in the world. The forge was an important supplier of high-quality iron forgings, including axles for the expanding Victorian railway network; and survived as a significant industrial operation into the early 20th century. (For more information, see www.topforge.co.uk).

The easiest way to reach the museum is to cross the river and follow the road round for another 300 yards. Then, to rejoin the route continue along the road past the bus stop and bear left over the next river bridge onto the signed path, which doubles as an access track, passing various buildings before reaching a line of terraced cottages facing some old garages. Here the walk along the riverside (see below) meets and the onward route bears up past the houses.

A pleasant alternative follows the river. Take the signed path immediately before the bridge, a few yards downhill from the pub on the opposite side of the road. After about 100 yards a waymark directs you left, away from the water's edge, up towards and onto the Trans Pennine Trail, whereby you can bear right and walk south (on an embankment then in a cutting) for several hundred yards until you pass under an overbridge, and 30 yards beyond come to a signpost and path junction (point C on map). However, arguably best of all is to continue on the riverside path and follow it round (with views over the river to the fishponds on the other bank) until it reaches the buildings and stables, where continuing ahead will allow you to overlook the garden exhibits of the Top Forge Museum across the river, reach the road and bear right for the museum. In

Huthwaite Hall

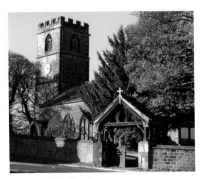

Wortley parish church

any event, the onward route from here, and for those who have reached here from the Top Forge, bears left or right respectively up past the terrace of houses, then enters and climbs a field with a pair of trees directly ahead and the old railway cutting to the left in the trees. This is a pleasantly rural stretch, although, as you climb, the noise of traffic on the Stockbridge bypass becomes more apparent. You come to a stone bridge over the old railway, and then walk down a slope to join the trail at a signpost and path junction (C ☺ 298994).

Here take the 'Timberland Trail', left, towards Finkle Street; and walk the short distance down to join, for the second time, the road close to the old Wortley Station, just a few yards from the flagged path you used to reach this point earlier in the day. Bear left and left again, and now it's simply a question of retracing your steps up the hill to Wortley, where you may have noticed earlier that everything is nice and compact. The **2 Wortley Arms** occupies a roadside position opposite the church; getting into it takes a bit of care given the fairly heavy traffic negotiating the two right-angled bends at this spot. Once safely across, you'll find a carefully modernised building of some distinction, making a good contribution to the townscape in this village, which is not short of decent architecture. Entry is via the revolving doors: bear left in the lobby for the small but comfortable floorboarded bar area. Note the extensive collection of

Sheffield Wednesday FC memorabilia on the wall. Three changing beers support local breweries such as Stancil and Bradfield. Food service takes a break between 2.30 and 5pm except at weekends.

Leaving the Wortley Arms, it's little more than a shuffle around the building to the right, passing the bus stop for Sheffield, to reach the entry to the **3 Wortley Men's Club**. Open each day from 2pm (but mid-week, check first by phoning ahead as it may sometimes be 4pm), this serial award winner (and CAMRA's 2015 National Club of the Year) is not to be missed. Formerly the library of the adjacent Wortley Hall estate, this attractive building has high ceilings in the lounge and a little snug at the side of the bar. Timothy Taylor's Landlord is the regular beer, complemented by two changing guests.

If you have time, a visit to Wortley Hall itself (whose entrance driveway is right outside the Wortley Men's Club) is strongly recommended. The splendid building has a fascinating history, facing ruin but then being rescued by an alliance of Trade and Labour movement societies after the Second World War, and now run co-operatively as an educational and holiday centre. The house is accompanied by formal gardens, and the nearby walled garden, now being restored and worked again with the help of volunteers, is remarkable. Furthermore, the bar, with real ale available, is open to visitors.

PUB INFORMATION

 BRIDGE INN
Cote Lane, Thurgoland, S35 7AE
0114 288 8829 • www.thurgolandbridgeinn.co.uk
Opening hours: 12 (4 Mon)-10 (11 Thu-Sat);
12-10 Sun

 WORTLEY ARMS
Halifax Road, Wortley, S35 7DB
0114 288 5218 • www.wortley-arms.co.uk
Opening hours: 12-11 (11.30 Fri; midnight Sat);
12-8.30 Sun

 WORTLEY MEN'S CLUB
Reading Room Lane, Wortley, S35 7DB
0114 288 2066 • www.wortleymensclub.co.uk
Opening hours: 2-11 Mon-Fri; 12-11 Sat & Sun

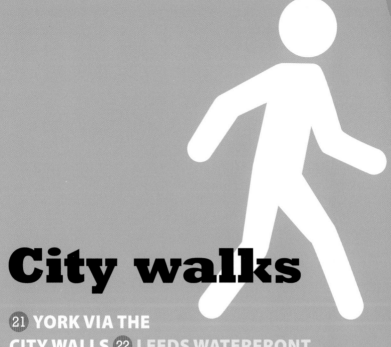

City walks

York via the City walls

York will come close to many people's idea of a dream place for a pub walk: oozing history and culture throughout, a well-preserved line of city walls to walk round, and a portfolio of interesting pubs, many with historic features, which showcase a wide range of old and new beers. To enjoy the city's pubs to the full, time planning your campaign will be well spent, since many pubs are inconveniently closed at times, and others like the wonderful little Blue Bell are victims of their own success in this tourist mecca and it's worth going out of your way to catch them at quieter times. As with other urban pub walks with numerous stops on the way this walk should be treated as a framework, for you to adapt as it suits.

▸ **Start/finish:** York railway station

▸ **Distance:** 4 miles (6.4km)

▸ **Key attractions:** York Minster; Historic city walls and architecture; National Railway Museum; Jorvik and other museums.

▸ **THE PUBS:** Royal Oak; Blue Bell; Rook & Gaskill; Phoenix; Swan; Golden Ball; Brigantes; Maltings; York Tap. Try also: Waggon & Horses

▸ **Timing tips:** Several of the pubs on this route are closed until late afternoon during the week so a weekend, or a late start on a long summer day is the best plan. Alternatively take a long break for sightseeing in the middle of the day, and split the pubs in two!

York Minster and Lendal Bridge from the city walls

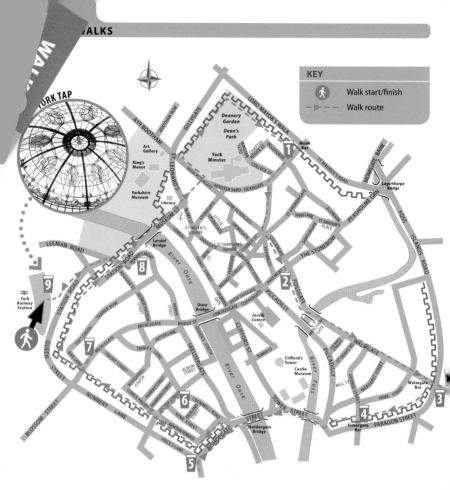

The Oak Room in the Royal Oak

This trail starts at York station, very close to the National Rail Museum which is in itself worth a lengthy visit particularly if you haven't been before. Leaving the station the city walls are across the road, bear left passing the Royal York hotel and in about 200 yards you can climb up onto the city walls from Station Road: cross the road and walk under them through the bridge and take the steps. Immediately a great view of the Minster opens up before you. York has the most complete medieval city walls still standing in England today, and they are constructed on the remains of earlier walls dating as far back as the Roman period. With some casualties they survived attempts by York Corporation to demolish them largely because of local opposition during the nineteenth century.

Walking towards the cathedral, take note of the Maltings on your right shortly before reaching the river at the Lendal Bridge. We'll call in here towards the end of the trail, but

The walls give an excellent vantage point for enjoying the city

if you want to sneak in early, jump ahead for the description. The Barker Tower adjacent to the steps as you descend to the bridge was built in the 14th century and used to control river traffic entering the city before the Lendal Bridge was opened in 1863. An iron chain was stretched across the river between this and the Lendal Tower opposite and boatmen had to pay a toll to cross it. The iron bridge carries the White Rose of York, the crossed keys of the Diocese of York and the lions of England.

Walk up Museum Street passing the Museum gardens (inside is the Yorkshire Museum and the remains of St Mary's Abbey church) to the Minster which dominates the forward view. No pub guide can do justice to the stupendous Minster so I won't even try; but you will have factored in time (and money!) to visit if you wish to do so.

"York is the second city in the kingdom"

THE NEW ROYAL GEOGRAPHICAL MAGAZINE, 1810

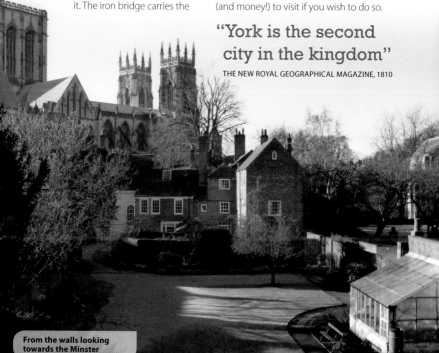

From the walls looking towards the Minster

The Blue Bell is an unspoilt gem and a must-visit

I do recommend the Dean's Park Garden alongside in its own right and for good external views of the Minster; then the best way to continue from the Minster grounds is to head down High Petergate to the Bootham Bar, one of the four main gates to the medieval city (in addition there were six postern or secondary gates).

Ascend the walls again here and walk in a clockwise direction towards the Monk's Bar on Goodramgate. I should explain that the word 'bar' here is not what you might hope or expect, simply a name for one of the old gateways to the medieval city! This is perhaps the finest surviving stretch of the walls, overlooking as it does the Dean's Park and the lovely gardens of the houses, notably the superb Treasurer's House, in the Minster Yard.

Descend at The Monk's Bar by the Richard III 'experience' and start down pretty Goodramgate and you'll see the first stop of the day, the **1 Royal Oak** in just 25 yards or so. This compact three room Tudor-style pub (almost completely

The Maltings boasts a bar made of old timber doors

rebuilt in the 1930s so ignore the usual tosh suggesting it's centuries old!) has recently had a sensitive restoration. This has seen the fitted bench seating restored to the little snug (on the front right), similar to that in the larger Oak Room (front left) with its terrazzo flooring and open fire. Food is available but at this time of day you'll be more interested in the range of beers, staples from Theakston including Old Peculier; Greene King's Abbot Ale, and up to three rotating guests.

A quiet corner of the Dean's Garden

Leaving the pub continue down Goodramgate (and note the left fork by the Cross Keys) which has its fair share of genuinely historic buildings, not least the timber framed and plastered Our Lady's Row cottages, built in 1316 and believed to be the oldest medieval 'jettied' houses (whose upper story protrudes or 'jetties' outwards) in England. Just beyond these entered through a narrow archway is Holy Trinity church, a lovely old (probably 12th century) gem now managed by the Churches Conservation Trust who care for otherwise redundant old churches.

Reaching King's Square, bear left passing York Brewery's Last Drop Inn, walk down narrow Colliergate and then straight over into even narrower Fossgate. Here a few yards along on the right and unmistakeable on account of the distinctive if dubious pink tiling outside stands one of York's many historic pub gems, the **2** **Blue Bell**. The interior of this largely unaltered early twentieth century rebuild of a workingman's pub is a joy to behold for its simple authenticity; and nationally recognised by its rare Grade II* listing. A narrow drinking lobby/corridor links the front and back rooms, and dark varnished matchboard survives throughout as does tiled flooring and good Edwardian glazing, screens and service hatches. It would be a 'must visit' even if you could only get Watney's Red

Barrel, but fortunately these days the beer range is better than ever with four regulars including two from Bradfield brewery and Rudgate's Ruby Mild complemented by three changing guests. If you can get here early in the day you've a better chance of missing the hordes of trippers…

If you're looking to lose some time sightseeing before tackling the late afternoon openers, now is probably the time to do this as the next pub is a good 10 minute stroll out of the city centre. Otherwise, suitably refreshed, continue down Fossgate and cross the eponymous river into Walmgate continuing to city walls at the Walmgate Bar. Carefully cross the ring road just outside the gate and a few doors up on the right of Lawrence St is the **3** **Rook & Gaskill**. This excellent freehouse takes its beers very seriously indeed and regularly has plaudits bestowed upon it by the local CAMRA branch. As you can read inside 'Gaskill' is not some rare falcon or other mythical bird but one of the last two men to be hanged in York, back in 1676. The long servery flanked by a good terrazzo floor dispenses an interesting and always changing range of beers: expect eight of these plus 2 or three traditional ciders on handpull and a range of decent 'craft' keg beers as well. Think long and hard before

Brigantes is a light and modern open-plan brasserie

Mason's Arms, and keep left now crossing first the Foss then the larger Ouse, in between which on a spur of land is the site of York Castle and its impressive keep, the Clifford's Tower, which survives. Beyond the Ouse bridge pick up the line of walls again to your immediate right. Do not ascend though since the next call is close at hand. At the next junction across the road you'll spot the **5 Swan**. The fairly plain frontage belies an interior which is one of the best-preserved and most interesting in York. The 1930's remodelling of the pub features a superb Yorkshire drinking lobby, one of the best survivors of this style anywhere (comparable with the Three Pigeons in Halifax, also in this volume); and two rooms lead off. The six beers (Saltaire Blonde, and Tetley and Taylor Landlord bitters plus guests) play only a supporting role alongside the fitted seating, terrazzo floors and lead glazed screens. Finally the urinals here are a must-visit (sorry ladies!) so plan ahead accordingly. The Slip Inn (further down the road from the Swan) is worth a visit if you have the capacity, but to continue the official route, either (to walk via the walls) return to the last road junction on the ring road (with Cromwell Road) to climb the walls and continue your clockwise tour as far as the next exit, at the Victoria Bar. An additional advantage of this high level route is the continuous view of handsome Victorian terraces on the right hand side, inside the walls, on this stretch. If walking by road just follow the main road round to your

missing this pub from your circuit. The **10 Waggon & Horses** across the road is an excellent alternative/addition, with several beers from owners Batemans and three guests in a traditional interior (but not open until 3pm during the week).

Walking back across the ring road gain the city walls via the steps by Walmgate Bar and head south-westwards along the wall-top, with modern housing inside the walls and more distant views of the Minster. At the Fishergate postern, these days a pedestrian gateway, climb down again to the pub right adjacent to and inside the walls. The **4 Phoenix** is aptly named since it has brought by to life in the last few years by owners who have brought the simple but historic two-roomed interior back to its best; although the name probably relates to a nearby but now long-gone foundry. There are five ales on tap here, check the web site for the current 'residents' and guests…

It's probably best now to stray down from the wall path and follow the road so head through the postern and bear right onto Paragon St., following it round to the right past the interesting-looking interwar

The Treasurer's House, Minster Yard

left on leaving the Swan until you reach the gate in a few minutes. Head at 90 degrees away from the walls towards the city for a couple of minutes to reach the **6 Golden Ball**. A lively street corner community hub, this traditional four-roomed pub is listed for its unspoilt internal layout. It also became York's first community co-operative pub back in 2012. Equally important it's a *Good Beer Guide* regular on account of its well-kept range of seven cask beers, mainly rotating guests alongside Yorkshire favourites like the ubiquitous Taylor Landlord.

Head back to the walls, and walk down to the next gate, the Micklegate Bar, which is the location of another museum. Again walk up inside the walls on Micklegate to **7 Brigantes** on the left in no time at all. Quiet a contrast from the last few pubs this, for it's a light and modern open-plan brasserie-style bar, but one with a first-class reputation for fine ales and good food. Ten handpumps dispense both regular beers

from Yorkshire breweries, and four guests. Continental beers and real cide are also on offer, and all available in combinations of third pint upwards.

We're now getting closer to the end of our marathon pub walk: if time presses (or if you visited the Maltings earlier), the best option to return to the station if to exit the Micklegate Bar and follow the roadside around the foot of the walls to arrive at the station and the York Tap (below) in a few minutes. Otherwise re-ascend the walls and walk along the top around past the station, descending where you first mounted the walls at the start of the walk; and then following the walls at their foot down to the **8 Maltings** which you looked down upon earlier. Possibly the most well-known of York's rich portfolio of real ale pubs, and far better than the grim black paint job bestowed upon the exterior suggests, the partially opened out interior of several drinking areas retains much

The York Tap is housed in the station's former tea room

...ter although some of it is ...nitely not original, such as ...e old timber doors (!) affixed to ...he ceiling and bar front. Expect regulars Black Sheep Bitter and York Guzzler to be joined by half a dozen guests from near and far with Roosters a favoured brewer.

Finally, return to York station where another in a growing list of notable railway station alehouses can be found. The **9 York Tap** is owned by Pivovar, who also have the Sheffield and Euston taps so they know a thing or two about beer. The building occupied by the Tap was originally opened in 1907 by the North Eastern Railway as the station's tea room. It subsequently housed a model railway but has been restored

The Maltings

to its former glory by Pivovar before being opened as the York Tap in 2011. They made such a lovely job of it that it won The Railway Heritage Trust Conservation Award in 2012. It's a fine place to enjoy a huge beer list: with

some eighteen cask beers and almost as many craft beers and ciders to choose from you're bound to find something you love here. And you can roll out the door almost straight onto the train, if you're going that way...

PUB INFORMATION

 ROYAL OAK
18 Goodramgate, York, YO1 7LG
01904 628869 • www.royaloakyork.co.uk
Opening hours: 10-midnight

 BLUE BELL
53 Fossgate, York, YO1 9TF
01904 654904
Opening hours: 11-11 Mon-Sat; 12-10.30 Sun

 ROOK & GASKILL
12 Lawrence Street, York, YO10 3WP
01904 655459 • www.rookandgaskillyork.co.uk
Opening hours: 4-midnight; 12-1am Fri & Sat

PHOENIX
75 George Street, YO1 9PT
01904 656401 • www.thephoenixinnyork.co.uk
Opening hours: 5-11 Mon-Thu; 4.30-11.30 Fri;
12.30-11.30 Sat; 2.30-11 Sun

...WAN
...ishopgate Street, York, YO23 1JH
...634968
...g hours: 4-11 (11.30 Thu; midnight Fri);
...ht Sat; 12-10.30 Sun

 GOLDEN BALL
2 Cromwell Road, York, YO1 6DU
01904 652211 • www.goldenballyork.co.uk
Opening hours: 5 (4 Fri; 12 Sat)-11.30; 12-11 Sun

 BRIGANTES
114 Micklegate, York, YO1 6JX
01904 675355
Opening hours: 12-11

 MALTINGS
Tanners Moat, York, YO1 6HU
01904 655387 • www.maltings.co.uk
Opening hours: 11-11; 12-10.30 Sun

 YORK TAP
Railway Station, Station Road, York, YO24 1AB
01904 659009
Opening hours: 10-11 (11.45 Fri & Sat); 11-11 Sun

Try also:

 WAGGON & HORSES
19 Lawrence Street, York, YO10 3BP •
01904 637478 • www.waggonandhorsesyork.com
Opening hours: 3-11.30; 12-midnight Fri & Sat; 12-11 Sun

Leeds waterfront

Central Leeds has undergone the sort of makeover that many other British inner cities have seen in the past 20 years, with the result that the old area of Holbeck around the head of the Leeds–Liverpool canal is almost unrecognisable. Some attractive waterside areas have been opened up to public access, and a number of fine old buildings rehabilitated, although others, like the once-wonderful Marshall's Mill, still wait their turn.

WALK
22

▸ **Start/finish:** Leeds station

▸ **Distance:** 1.8 miles (3.02 km) for full circuit

▸ **Key attractions:** Leeds–Liverpool canal regeneration; nationally important pub interiors; Marshall's Mill (Grade II listed); Tower Works 'campaniles'; Leeds Industrial Museum

▸ **THE PUBS:** Hop, Pour House, Midnight Bell, Cross Keys, Northern Monk Refectory, Grove Inn, Adelphi, Whitelock's Ale House

CALLS LANDING

Waterfront regeneration in Leeds city centre

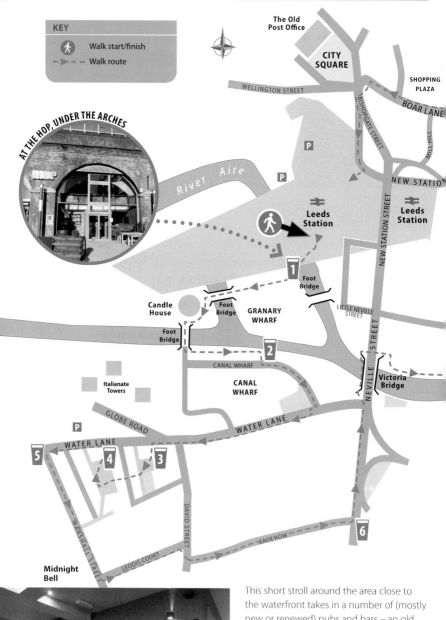

KEY

👤 Walk start/finish

⇢⇢⇢ Walk route

The Old Post Office

CITY SQUARE

SHOPPING PLAZA

WELLINGTON STREET

BISHOPGATE STREET

BOAR LANE

MILL HILL

NEW STATION

AT THE HOP, UNDER THE ARCHES

River Aire

P

P

NEW STATION STREET

Leeds Station

Leeds Station

1 Foot Bridge

LITTLE NEVILLE STREET

Candle House

Foot Bridge

GRANARY WHARF

Foot Bridge

NEVILLE STREET

2

CANAL WHARF

Victoria Bridge

Italianate Towers

CANAL WHARF

GLOBE ROAD

WATER LANE

P

WATER LANE

5

4

3

DAVID STREET

BACK ROW

6

MARSHALL STREET

LEODIS COURT

Midnight Bell

This short stroll around the area close to the waterfront takes in a number of (mostly new or renewed) pubs and bars – an old classic in the Grove – and can be lengthened by taking in a couple of CAMRA's 'Real Heritage Pubs' in the vicinity. The pubs are very close together and the good variety of styles and ambience allows you to pick and choose easily.

TURK'S HEAD YARD

8

RINITY
LEEDS

DUNCAN STREET

Treweyan
Square

LOWER BRIGGATE

VIADUCT STREET

HEATON'S COURT

CALL LANE

BLAYD'S YARD

Leeds
Bridge

GN STREET

7

WATER LANE

er Aire

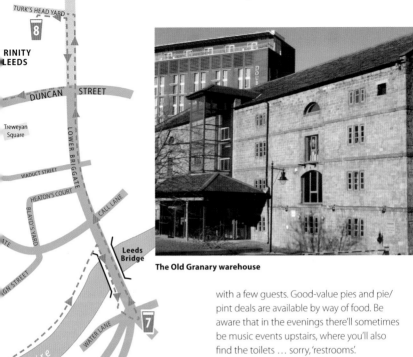

The Old Granary warehouse

with a few guests. Good-value pies and pie/pint deals are available by way of food. Be aware that in the evenings there'll sometimes be music events upstairs, where you'll also find the toilets … sorry, 'restrooms'.

Continue by bearing right and swing round the circular 'Candle House' block to cross the Leeds–Liverpool Canal by the pretty old canal office. A pleasant canal-side

Leeds railway station will have a new southern entrance by the time you read this, and this will be the best choice to access the start of the walk, bringing you out right by the waterside in the so-called Holbeck Urban Village. You'll arrive in the Granary Wharf area close to the junction of the canal with the River Aire as it disappears under the station. Towering above you is the 'Dalek' – or Bridgwater Place to give it its official title – the tallest building in the city. From the footbridge facing the new entrance, walk westwards through to a small square, where the City Inn ahead offers great views from the Skylounge at the top (if you can bear the corporate clients swanning around). Across to the right, occupying a couple of the railway arches, is the first pub stop of the day, the **Hop**. Yet another new venture by the ambitious Ossett brewery, the horseshoe-shaped interior is a good two-storey conversion. The beers are mainly as you'd expect from Ossett's mainly very blonde portfolio,

Leeds old and new – from the Hop

walk sets off from here down towards Leeds Industrial Museum and other goodies if you have the time, whilst prominent in the view here are the 'campaniles', the two towers once part of the now-derelict Tower Works. The smaller one, built in 1864, with its pretty Italianate top, is modelled on the Lamberti tower in Verona; whilst the function of the other, built 25 years later and modelled on the campanile at Florence cathedral, was to collect iron dust.

Tower Works campanile

Across the bridge bear sharp left onto the cobbled towpath, which leads in 100 yards to the **2 Pour House**, right on the waterside by the lock separating the Aire and the canal. Dating to about 1775, this handsome stone building was built by the canal company as a granary warehouse. The Pour House occupies a later extension of the building and has a modern interior, which is pretty food-orientated, but offers four cask beers and a pleasant waterside terrace for those warm days.

The start of the Leeds-Liverpool canal near the Pour House

Walk up to Water Lane and bear right, crossing over when the coast is clear. Cross David Street, and just a little further on is the next pub, the **3 Midnight Bell**. Barely five years in business, Leeds Brewery's Holbeck flagship already looks and feels a good deal more mature. As is now *de rigueur*, a long array of handpulls dispense three or four Leeds beers and a similar number of supporting guests, with all-day food available. This whole block in a former industrial area has undergone extensive renovation, and the pleasant rear courtyard allows one to take in the atmosphere: a modern take on the serving hatch opens onto this courtyard. In fact, the rear exit is a good way to reach the next pub just a few doors down the street, as you can walk through the backyard, bearing right through to Foundry Square via Saw Mill Yard and the back entrance to the **4 Cross Keys** in another enclosed square with plenty of seating. Inside, the Keys is a very good renovation, which has successfully created a traditional, pubby atmosphere. Two rooms wrap around the servery, each with a multi-fuel stove, and displaying a variety of floor coverings from stone to quarry tile to rustic floorboards. It's part of the North Bar chain, so expect up to four mainly local beers and an impressive selection of bottled beers, notably from Germany, Belgium and the United States. Food is of good quality.

If you like the idea of new uses for old buildings, then the next port of call is one for you. Leaving the Cross Keys by the front door this time, bear left and swing round the corner into Marshall Street, which was once the centre of the important Leeds flax industry. A large brick mill dominates the view up the street, but, before you reach it, swing into the yard on your right and look for the old flax store, a former warehouse that is home to one of the area's latest ventures, the **5 Northern Monk Refectory**. To call the décor minimalist is probably about right: you need to walk up a spartan staircase and pass the communal toilets to access the first floor bar, and once inside think 'refectory' to picture it. This is the brewery tap for the new Northern Monk micro, which specialises in modern and interesting, though mainly pretty strong, 'craft' keg-style beers. The four cask lines offer mainly local guests from the likes of Saltaire. Beer prices are every bit as lofty as the accommodation, while there's an ambitious food menu including a good range of vegan and vegetarian dishes, all at reasonable prices.

Inside the Cross Keys

Continuing up Marshall Street leads to perhaps the architectural highlight of the day, albeit one in serious need of TLC. The Egyptian-style Temple Works up on the right beyond the brick mill was in its time the centre of the flax industry, but is a fine example of the Victorian skill in promoting art and style via industry. Sadly neglected today, one can but hope that a suitable modern use can be found for this giant ghost of our industrial past. By contrast, its surroundings are as dismal an advert for modern commercial mediocrity as you could hope to find: bear down Leodis Court and more or less straight across into Back Row with the 'Dalek' acting as your beacon.

Having completed a tour of five of the most modern drinking holes in this whole volume, the last of the entries in the Holbeck area is as traditional and old-fashioned as they get. The **6 Grove Inn** is a well-known 19th-century multi-room beerhouse, very humble in structure but a rare survivor these days. It also retains the Yorkshire 'drinking corridor', which interests the sociologists of beer culture – though at busy times loitering in it might not be popular with fellow imbibers seeking out the rear rooms. As for beer, suffice to say that you will not want for choice, and one can hope that the relatively new owners will uphold the reputation for quality as well as variety that the Grove has earned.

It would be no shame to call it a day at this point and make your way over the bridge back to nearby Leeds station – but for lovers of high-quality pub interiors, the final two pubs, taken in on a slightly longer extension of the route, are a must, particularly if you haven't visited either before.

To reach them, cross the Aire as if heading back to the station and, crossing the road carefully, head down the steps to the riverside path and walk downstream, passing more regenerated buildings with the gigantic ASDA HQ staring at you from the south bank. I'm told that, if built, the Leeds terminal of high-speed rail link HS2 will require its demolition, perhaps the best argument I've yet heard for the project! Climb up to street level at handsome Leeds Bridge and re-cross the river to the **7 Adelphi** on a bold corner site. Built in 1901 in the generous and lavish style of the late Victorian period, this multi-roomed palace has survived remarkably well despite a few less sympathetic modern alterations. From a central lobby with its mosaic floor

Drinking passage in the Adelphi

four rooms lead off. There's plenty of tilework, etched glass in good-quality screens, and rich mahogany fittings throughout to enjoy while you're sampling from a range of four to five cask beers.

Re-cross the river again and stroll up into the city centre. Numerous good buildings from Leeds' Victorian heyday have survived to admire as you do, particularly around the junction with Boar Lane (note the tower of Holy Trinity church to the left, and the distinctive Corn Exchange to the right as you cross directly into the pedestrianised stretch of Briggate). Some 100 yards up on the left look out for sign leading down an alleyway

to **8 Whitelock's Ale House**. This legendary Leeds institution opened as the Turk's Head in 1715, and was acquired in 1880 by the Whitelock family, who were responsible for the layout we see today. Tilework, mirrors and dark woodwork abound throughout the long and narrow building; and note the rare part-marble, part-copper bar top. John Betjeman described it as the very heart of Leeds and, indeed, in its 1930s heyday it would have been difficult to disagree. It's still a must-see for lovers of pub heritage, and these days it offers a wider range of cask beers alongside the food for which the 'First City Luncheon Bar' is probably more well known.

It's a short walk back to Leeds station along Boar Lane, having turned right past Holy Trinity church.

Tiles and marble inside Whitelock's Ale House

PUB INFORMATION

 HOP
Granary Wharf, Dark Neville Street, Leeds, LS1 4BR
0113 243 9854 • www.thehop-leeds.co.uk
Opening hours: 12-midnight

 POUR HOUSE
Canal Wharf, Water Lane, Holbeck, Leeds, LS11 5PS
07816 481492 • www.thepourhouseleeds.co.uk
Opening hours: 11.30-11.30 (12.30am Fri & Sat)

 MIDNIGHT BELL
101 Water Lane, Holbeck, Leeds, LS11 5QN
0113 244 5044 • www.midnightbell.co.uk
Opening hours: 12-11 (midnight Fri & Sat)

 CROSS KEYS
107 Water Lane, Holbeck, Leeds, LS11 5WD
0113 243 3711 • www.the-crosskeys.com
Opening hours: 12-11 (midnight Fri & Sat); 12-11.30 Sun

5 NORTHERN MONK REFECTORY
The Old Flax Store, Marshalls Mill, Holbeck, Leeds, LS11 9YJ
0113 243 6430
www.northernmonkbrewco.com/the-refectory
Opening hours: 8-midnight (1am Fri); 10-1am Sat; 10-midnight Sun

 GROVE INN
Back Row, Holbeck, Leeds, LS11 5PL
0113 244 1440 • www.thegroveinn.com
Opening hours: 12-11 (midnight Fri & Sat)

 ADELPHI
3-5 Hunslet Road, Leeds, LS10 1JQ
0113 245 6377 • www.theadelphileeds.co.uk
Opening hours: 12-11 (12.30 Fri & Sat)

 WHITELOCK'S ALE HOUSE
Turk's Head Yard, Leeds, LS1 6HB
0113 242 3368 • www.whitelocksleeds.com
Opening hours: 11-midnight (1am Fri & Sat); 11-11 Sun

Sheffield: Kelham Island & the 'valley of beer'

- **Start:** Sheffield railway station or Bamforth Street tram stop
- **Finish:** Sheffield railway station
- **Distance:** Approx 4 miles (6.5 km) to and from Shalesmoor
- **Key attractions:** Kelham Island Museum; Millennium and Graves art galleries; Abbeydale Industrial Hamlet
- **THE PUBS:** New Barrack Tavern, Hillsborough Hotel, Shakespeare's Ale & Cider House, Kelham Island Tavern, Fat Cat, Riverside, Gardeners Rest, Wellington, Sheffield Tap. Try also: Harlequin

Sheffield's Don Valley has become well known to many discerning imbibers as the 'valley of beer' for its ample array of attractive watering holes arranged conveniently along the valley and close to the 'super-tram' routes. It's fair to give a special mention to the pioneering Fat Cat at Kelham Island, now in its 25th year; but it's now joined by other award-winning venues, making this an urban route to enjoy whether you choose to go the whole hog or select from the riches on offer. I've added to the itinerary the excellent Sheffield Tap, another in Yorkshire's growing portfolio of fine railway station bars and not to be missed. It's easy to omit some pubs without it being too far to the next.

The 'Riverside' is aptly named...

The route starts at Bamforth Street tram stop. If you're starting from the station, both the Blue (Malin Bridge) and Yellow (Middlewood) routes will do, alighting at Bamforth Street. If you're on a bus, it's Langsett Road/Channing Street. If you're in the city centre then a tram from the Shalesmoor stop will take you to Bamforth Street.

Alighting from the tram or bus, walk ahead another 75 yards or so and cross over to walk down Burton Street. A left/right dogleg near the foot of the hill allows you to emerge on Penistone Road almost outside the 1 **New Barrack Tavern**. A rather austere looking 1930s building, it has a multi-room layout comprising a large lounge, with smaller rooms in support, and a pleasant beer garden at the rear. Now part of the successful Castle Rock estate, the pub offers not just staples from the Nottingham brewer's portfolio (including seasonals), but guests from Acorn and Bradfield. Home-cooked food is available daily, with roasts on Sundays. Note the etched windows in favour of 'Gilmour's Windsor Ales & Stouts', this is one of many pubs in the area that still carry vestiges of the old Sheffield brewer.

Return to the Langsett Road and take the tram one stop south (or the bus to Primrose Hill). Walk on another 50 yards to the left-hand bend, where on the corner sits the 2 **Hillsborough Hotel**. Formerly known as the Wellington and therefore nicknamed the 'Top Wellie' by locals – the 'Bottom Wellie' (see below) is further down the road – this is another uncompromising exterior in deep red brick, but which conceals a warmer heart with sofas and cosy corners inside. The cellar in this privately owned hotel is home to the Wood Street brewery: expect at least four beers from down below on the bar, alongside guest beers from local and other independent breweries. Home-cooked meals are served throughout the day, and again brewery history fans will appreciate more old Gilmour's brewery windows.

After the Hillsborough Hotel, it's possible to vary the 'official' itinerary by making for the Gardener's Rest if it's open (it doesn't open until 3pm Monday to Thursday). If you take this option, you'll need to consult the map and the

The multi-award winning winning Kelham Island Tavern

route description further down, taking in the pubs in a different order.

The main route, however, involves a tram or bus back down to Shalesmoor; and this time, having alighted, look across to the eastern side of the busy A61 and you'll spot the attractive faience-tiled exterior of the Ship Inn. Make your way carefully across the roads to the Ship – which is currently closed with a very uncertain future, but

this super little place has won more awards than almost any other UK pub, and these are proudly displayed outside. What is less well known is that the place was rescued from dereliction around the turn of the millennium. The L-shaped interior is surprisingly compact, but in summer the enjoyable beer garden is open and offers the many visitors more space to enjoy the excellent beers. There's around a dozen cask ales to choose from, mostly guests but with a few fixtures including Acorn's reliable Barnsley Bitter. Food is straightforward and sensible pub grub.

Coming out of the Kelham Island Tavern you won't work up much of a thirst before encountering the next stop, since you can practically see it back across the A61, thanks to the cleared plots along Russell Street at the time of writing. To get there, continue along Russell Street, cross the A61 and aim for **4** **Shakespeare's Ale & Cider House**

KEY

🚶 Walk start/finish

Walk route

Alternative route

NEEPSEND

River Don

LITTLE KELHAM

SHALESMOOR

SAINT VINCENT'S

DEREK DOOLEY WAY

WICKER A61

SAVILE STREET

Park Square

VIEW FROM THE SHEFFIELD TAP

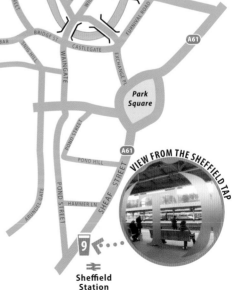

the exterior is admirable nonetheless, with tiled adverts for long-defunct Tomlinson's Anchor ales. Walk down the street (Dun Fields) leading down into Kelham Island from the Ship. At the foot, noting the handsome, listed exterior of the old Green Lane works capped with its clock tower, bear right and walk through an area undergoing a good deal of regeneration.

In less than a minute you'll come upon the welcoming façade of the **3** **Kelham Island Tavern** ahead of you, just past the popular Grind café, itself an indication of the regeneration of this area (see box). The pub itself may need little introduction to many, as

Sheffield Station

Colourful breweriania in the Shakespeare

whose gable is adorned with a helpful sign, just around the corner in Gibraltar Street. Refurbished and re-opened as a free house just five years ago, it's a welcome addition to the beer valley circuit. Originally a coaching inn, the archway to the yard has now been incorporated into the pub and you can sit in the former passageway and admire a fine collection of breweriana; three other rooms are arranged around the central servery. Up to eight changing guest beers are available, together with real cider, an extensive bottled beer list and more than 100 whiskies. Also in the old coachway alley is an interesting magazine article by four PhD students who (hopefully not with public money!) researched and ranked all Sheffield's pubs 'scientifically' (and guess which one came out top?).

To continue the circuit retrace your steps back towards the Kelham Island Tavern, and once again, thanks to current regeneration, you can see the famous **5 Fat Cat** sitting down below on Alma Street just a stone's throw in the other direction. If you can't walk straight across the derelict plot to it, take the first right beyond the Kelham Island Tavern. The now legendary pub, once known as the Alma, dates back to 1850 but was bought by two 'free spirits' in 1981. One of them was Dave Wickett, a pioneer of small

breweries and independent pubs. The idea was to provide an alternative to the pubs owned by the big breweries, so a new range of beers, many but not all from small independent breweries, was promoted. In 1989, Dave bought out his partner and set up the Kelham Island brewery alongside the pub: a commonplace occurrence today but real swashbuckling stuff in those days. He kept things small and manageable, and both pub and brewery collected numerous awards. Sadly Dave died of cancer in 2012, but the Fat Cat is part of his legacy, and his son continues the good work at the brewery. As for the pub, it continues as Dave nurtured it: a traditional no-frills but homely interior, plenty of beer choice, and all-day food with a good range of vegetarian and gluten-free dishes. For all these reasons, the Fat Cat is to me, and surely to many visitors, the nucleus of the Sheffield 'Beer Valley' circuit.

For those wishing to take in a visit to the industrial museum, this is the time to do it; either way, the easiest way to get to the next pub on the circuit is to head down Alma Street to join the busy road at the bottom. Now bear left, and before you even cross the Don you'll see the little terrace of the **6 Riverside** hanging onto the east bank of the river. The interior has been opened out in a modern idiom apart from a separate room to the right as you enter; furnishings include a mix of comfortable sofas and armchairs together with more spartan canteen-style tables and chairs. The two house beers come from the nearby Sheffield Brewery Company, and are complemented by a changing selection of guest ales, mostly from local breweries. Be prepared for intrusive musak, but in good weather the terrace/garden is a pleasant haven to enjoy the beers. Food is of the burgers and fries-with-everything variety.

Hardcore beer-walk aficionados have the option of taking in an additional pub on leaving the Riverside – once again it's visible across the racetrack of a road outside. The spacious **10 Harlequin** is housed in a traditional building and offers another very wide selection of cask ales, cider and 'craft' beers such that you are guaranteed to find something to hit the spot. It's certainly recommended if you have the time and capacity!

Ship (currently closed)

When you've had your fill, retrace your steps across the traffic lights, and now bear right onto the riverside path alongside the former Neepsend Rolling Mills. An information board explains the layout of the site here, one of many similar mills that existed in this part of the city at one time. Continue along the pleasant path for about 250 yards, passing modern apartments on the left, while across the river lies a museum of semi-dereliction, quite attractive in its own way, until you reach Ball Street Bridge, now kitted out in white and green paint, with the painted gable end of the old 'Alfred Beckett Steel, Saw and File Works'. Cross the bridge

The punishing circuit continues by heading north along Neepsend Lane from the Riverside (unless, of course, you diverted earlier to take in the Gardener's Rest). There is a bus stop in 50 yards (First Group service 53 runs every 10 minutes during the week, less often at weekends) if you don't fancy the 10–12-minute walk. A short distance beyond the Rutland Road crossroads and traffic lights, and again on the riverside, stands the **7 Gardener's Rest**. Badly damaged by flooding in 2007, this bright and welcoming pub, tucked in among industrial buildings, re-opened two years later and serves as the tap for the nearby Sheffield Brewery. Expect at least four beers from this excellent micro but plenty of guests from other small independents, too. The clean, bright interior has retained the cosy lounge. The main bar area features art exhibitions and live music at weekends, and has a restored bar billiards table. To the rear is a conservatory leading to the atmospheric beer garden overlooking the River Don.

KELHAM ISLAND

Sheffield's original alehouse and brewery

Kelham Island is the name given to the district below Shalesmoor and along the River Don. Formerly it was an important industrial area, the 'island' deriving from the building of a mill race or 'goit' fed from the River Don to serve the water-powered workshops. Sadly, as usual, the industries are largely no more, and in their place the Kelham Island Industrial Museum is there to remember them; some of the industrial buildings, notably the listed Brooklyn and Green Lane works, have survived, but regeneration is in full swing, and (almost inevitably) Sheffield's council bosses have included Kelham Island in the current obsession for naming 'quarters' in cities across the UK. Sheffield has a lot more than four... For the beer tourist, however, the name is synonymous with the Kelham Island brewery, opened in 1990 adjacent the Fat Cat pub; and happily both pub and brewery are still in rude health.

and continue ahead, crossing almost straight over at the cross-roads, which brings you out by the Shalesmoor junction.

By now the **Wellington** should be open. Now reverted to its former name (hence the 'Bottom Wellie') after a spell as the Cask & Cutler, it remains a popular two-roomed street-corner local and champions a range of beers from small independent brewer-ies. The 10 handpumps always offer a stout or porter, a cider and at least three beers from the previously in-house Little Ale Cart brewery, which has recently relocated to larger premises, having outgrown the old brewery adjacent to the secluded beer garden. A range of continental bottled beers is also available.

After a punishing, if superlative circuit such as this, it's good to know that transport is at hand almost outside the door; and for those with the stamina, a tram ride back to the station means a visit to one of the

Sheffield Tap

country's best-loved railway alehouses: the **Sheffield Tap**. Originally built in 1904 as the First Class refreshment rooms, the main bar area has been the subject of an award-winning restoration and retains many original features. It opened in 2009, and in 2013 the on-site Tapped Brewery opened in the former dining room. The brewery can be viewed behind a glass screen. As with the Wellington, handpumps make it into double figures and you'll be bamboozled with choice to round off one of the country's great pub trawls.

PUB INFORMATION

 NEW BARRACK TAVERN
601 Penistone Road, Hillsborough, Sheffield, S6 2GA
0114 234 9148
Opening hours: 5 (11 Wed & Thu)-11; 11-midnight Fri & Sat; 12-11 Sun

 HILLSBOROUGH HOTEL
54-58 Langsett Road, Hillfoot, Sheffield, S6 2UB
0114 232 2100 • www.hillsborough-hotel.co.uk
Opening hours: 12-11 (midnight Fri & Sat)

SHAKESPEARE'S ALE & CIDER HOUSE
146-148 Gibraltar Street, Kelham Island, Sheffield, S3 8UB
0114 275 5959 • www.shakespeares-sheffield.co.uk
Opening hours: 12-midnight (1am Fri & Sat)

 KELHAM ISLAND TAVERN
62 Russell Street, Kelham Island, Sheffield, S3 8RW
0114 272 2482 • www.kelhamtavern.co.uk
Opening hours: 12-midnight

 FAT CAT
23 Alma Street, Kelham Island, Sheffield, S3 8SA
0114 249 4801 • www.thefatcat.co.uk
Opening hours: 12-11 (midnight Fri & Sat)

 RIVERSIDE
1 Mowbray Street, Kelham Island, Sheffield, S3 8EN
0114 281 3621 • www.riversidesheffield.co.uk
Opening hours: 12-11 (midnight Fri & Sat)

 GARDENER'S REST
105 Neepsend Lane, Neepsend, Sheffield, S3 8AT
0114 272 4978
Opening hours: 3 (12 Thu)-11; 12-midnight Fri & Sat; 12-11 Sun

 WELLINGTON
1 Henry Street, Kelham Island, Sheffield, S3 7EQ
0114 249 2295
Opening hours: 12-11; 12-3.30, 7-10.30 Sun

 SHEFFIELD TAP
Platform 1b, Sheffield Station, Sheaf Street, Sheffield, S1 2BP
0114 273 7558 • www.sheffieldtap.com
Opening hours: 11-11; 10-midnight Fri & Sat

Try also:

 HARLEQUIN
108 Nursery Street, Kelham Island, Sheffield, S3 8GG
0114 249 4181 • www.theharlequinpub.co.uk
Opening hours: 12-11 (11.30 Thu & Fri; midnight Sat)

Historic Beverley

Once one of the largest dozen towns in the country, Beverley is now all the better for having been somewhat bypassed by 'progress'. Its former importance partly explains the presence of the must-see Minster (which has been called Yorkshire's finest building) and the impressive church of St Mary, along with its imposing market square lined with fine buildings. An eclectic range of good pubs large and small, including what is billed as Yorkshire's first micropub, makes for an interesting ale trail, and in the White Horse Beverley boasts one of the classic unspoilt old pub interiors of England. Allow an hour to enjoy the Minster before heading into the town centre.

WALK 24

▶ **Start/finish:** Beverley railway station (or bus station)

▶ **Access:** Frequent trains from Hull

▶ **Distance:** 2.5 miles (4 km) from and to station

▶ **Key attractions:** Beverley Minster; Treasure House Museum & Art Gallery; St Mary's church; North Bar gate and market cross; interior of White Horse pub

▶ **THE PUBS:** Dog & Duck, White Horse (Nellie's), Chequers Micropub, Woolpack, Tiger Inn. Try also: Cornerhouse (opening restrictions)

▶ **Timing tips:** The first two pubs on the trail open at 11am, so an early start works well; Beverley also makes an excellent base for visiting nearby Hull, so both pub trails could be done in a weekend. Once again, avoid Mondays when more than one pub is shut all day

Beverley's former Dominican Friary, over-looked by the Minster

Norwood Park

WYLIES ROAD

Recommended detour

6

2

North Bar Gate

NORTH BAR WITHIN

St Mary's Church

HENGATE

WHITE HORSE, BETTER KNOWN AS NELLIE'S

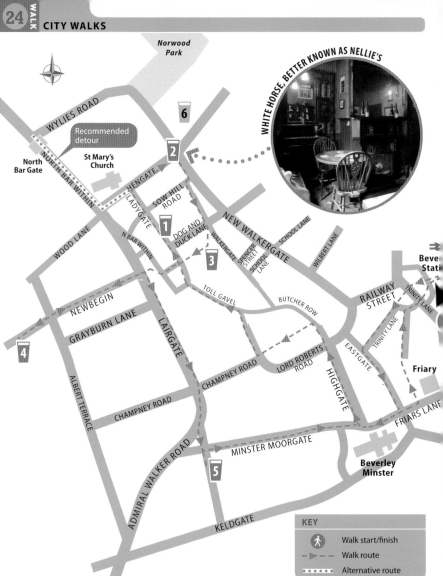

SOW HILL ROAD

LADYGATE

1

DOG AND DUCK LANE

NEW WALKERGATE

SCHOOL LANE

WILBERT LANE

WOOD LANE

N BAR WITHIN

3

WALKERGATE

SPENCER STREET

SCHOOL LANE

Beve Stati

NEWBEGIN

GRAYBURN LANE

LAIRGATE

TOLL GAVEL

BUTCHER ROW

RAILWAY STREET

TRINITY LANE

TRINITY LANE

4

ALBERT TERRACE

CHAMPNEY ROAD

CHAMPNEY ROAD

LORD ROBERTS ROAD

EASTGATE

HIGHGATE

Friary

FRIARS LANE

ADMIRAL WALKER ROAD

MINSTER MOORGATE

5

Beverley Minster

KELDGATE

KEY

🚶 Walk start/finish

— ▶ — Walk route

•••••• Alternative route

🚶 However you arrive in Beverley, I recommend starting with a leisurely look around the Minster (see box), regarded by many as Yorkshire's finest building. From the station make your way down Trinity Lane (45 degrees to your left when exiting the station) and Eastgate. It's a 10-minute walk south from the bus station.

From the Minster, the direct route into the town centre is via Highgate, which leads to the small square known as Wednesday Market. Cross into the pedestrianised Butcher Row, passing the Queen's Head and, by the Tourist Office, turn left into Well Lane. Now, depending upon time and inclination, you can take a small detour (before heading up Cross Street on the right) to the Treasure House Museum & Art Gallery straight ahead (the conical tower just beyond the Magistrates Court). There are enjoyable

St Mary's church roof

The White Horse is an unspoilt heritage pub

displays on local history and folk life of the East Riding, as well as a very popular café. Admission is free.

Cross Street leads past the handsome Guildhall and, via shop-lined Toll Gavel, into the main square of Beverley and Saturday Market. Make your way towards the street running to the right of the old Corn Exchange (now Brown's), unless you first wish to drop in, now or later, to the excellent second-hand bookshop up Dyer's Lane, leading off the square to the right. Just beyond Brown's on Ladygate is the first stop of the day: the **Dog & Duck**. A 1930s pub, it retains something of its former three-roomed layout and is none the worse for a somewhat old-fashioned atmosphere. The main room adjacent the bar has a brick fireplace and unusual bentwood seating. On the bar itself are half a dozen ales with Yorkshire 'usual suspects' including Taylor's Golden Best, Black Sheep Best and Copper Dragon Golden Pippin, alongside a couple of guests. Good-value lunches are a feature here, and it's worth noting that the place has several guest rooms for bed and

The North Bar

breakfast, should you be looking for a beer base for your stay.

Leaving the Dog & Duck and continuing up Ladygate to the junction, the next pub is very close by; but, if you have a few minutes, I recommend a visit across the street to St Mary's church, which, save for being somewhat overshadowed by the Minster, is a splendid church in its own right with some fine architecture inside and out. And, around to the north from the church, the attractive street known as North Bar Within – which leads up to North Bar itself, the old gate to the town – is an enjoyable little detour.

Either way, the route continues by bearing east from Ladygate onto Hengate and walking down towards the traffic lights (beware the narrow pavement). The long frontage just before the lights is the unassuming exterior to one of Britain's great pub interiors, that of the **White Horse**, better known as 'Nellie's' after the redoubtable licensee, whose family had the pub for many decades before it was sold to current owners, Sam Smith, in 1975. In those days, apart from

Inside the Cornerhouse

The Market Cross and St Mary's church

Nellie and her sisters, the main bar was men only, but a warmer welcome is extended to all nowadays! Despite some alterations since those days, the pub has kept its remarkable character with dark atmospheric rooms connected by old corridors. The front snug and small parlour are particularly unspoilt. Despite what modernisers say, the pub seems popular with young and old alike. As usual with Sam's, the only hand-pulled beer is Old Brewery Bitter, so I am not allowed to recommend the keg stout (!); but whatever you choose, this pub is not to be missed!

From Nellie's, swing to the right at the traffic lights. If you're walking the route at the weekend or after 5pm Tuesday to Friday, the **6** **Cornerhouse** opposite offers the

largest range of cask ales in Beverley, and real cider, in a gastro-pub environment; Yorkshire breweries feature prominently in an extensive changing list, and it's well worth popping in to sample the wares (and at weekends breakfast until 1pm, if you want to soak up some of that alcohol!)

Otherwise or afterwards, continue south past the bus station down busy New Walkergate – but only as far as the fork in 150 yards, where old Walkergate bears off right protected by pedestrian bollards. And almost opposite the Registry Office turn right again into Swaby's Yard, where you'll immediately see the welcome sign of the **3** **Chequers Micropub**. I don't want to try and define a micropub, but they say it is Yorkshire's first; what we *can* say is that this little place is a real gem inside, and the atmosphere far more pubby than you might have expected from external appearances. Relaxed conversation takes place against a backdrop of a changing array of up to five interesting cask beers from near and far, recorded by the dazzling display of pump clips running up the stairs. Expect in addition half a dozen ciders/perries, but be aware that sometimes the pub closes

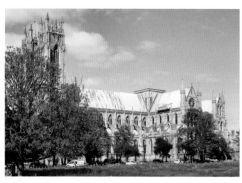

Beverley Minster

early if the evenings are quiet. All in all, it's a very welcome addition to Beverley's real ale portfolio and not to be missed.

You can snake through back to Saturday Market via Swaby's Yard and Dyer's Lane (passing the aforementioned second-hand bookshop), and this time head across to the far side of the square. From here, either sneak through the short alley (if you spot it) with the lovely name of Narrow Racket; or turn left on the corner into even shorter

Old Waste, and left again into Lairgate to reach Newbegin opposite the exit to Narrow Racket. Keep walking down Newbegin and across into Westwood Road, lined with handsome Victorian villas, to reach in a very few minutes the **4** **Woolpack**.

Having been built as a pair of cottages, the Woolpack became a pub around 1830, later adding its own brewhouse and stables. It's now a Marston's house serving beers from their stable, including one or two from

BEVERLEY MINSTER

Beverley Minster was originally founded as a monastery in the 8th century, but the Early English-style church one sees today dates primarily to the 13th and 14th centuries. It was a wealthy college church until the mid-16th century, when it was suppressed and reduced to the status of a parish church. Today, following major restoration work by Sir George Gilbert Scott and others, the building exists as a subordinate

in ecclesiastical terms to York, but many would argue that it is only subordinate in size and not in the splendour of its architecture, and is a cathedral in every aspect except status. Inside there are several treasures, including the superb Norman nave, leading to the great 15th-century east window, which still contains much of its original medieval stained glass. High-quality carvings in oak and in stone are

complemented by polished Purbeck marble columns and elaborately decorated tombs. Don't miss the massive Norman font with its astonishing canopy, a confection of carved scrolls and cherub heads; nor the organ screen designed by Scott but carved by a local man, James Elwell.

▼ **Beverley minster interior** ▶ **Stained glass detail**

The Tiger Inn's distinctive frontage   **The Woolpack was built as a pair of cottages**

Jennings, and a guest. The place has been opened out, but a lovely little snug with fitted bench seating and a tiled floor survives on the right, with its own serving hatch to the bar, albeit widened out a bit at some point. Good-quality food is served lunchtimes and evenings in this pleasant local.

Return to the junction with Lairgate, and this time turn right again to set out for the last pub of the tour. In about five minutes, when the main road veers to the right as you walk alongside a green, Lairgate continues straight ahead as a backwater and you'll see the sign and distinctive gable of the **5 Tiger Inn** well before you get there. The noteworthy frontage has some interesting carved timbers and points to a building of some antiquity, although it was revamped in the 1930s by the then owners, Darley's brewery. The public bar (on the right upon entry) and the rear parlour are the most atmospheric remaining rooms; and you'll see some now-rare matchboard ceilings, after, of course, you've chosen from Timothy Taylor's Landlord, Wychwood Hobgoblin and a couple of guest beers. Like the Woolpack before it, the Tiger Inn is also a popular destination for dining both at lunchtime and in the evenings.

To return to base, retrace your steps as far as Minster Moorgate, the first right turn in 30 yards, and head back to the Minster, where Highgate will return you to the town centre or, continuing via Eastgate and Trinity Lane, to the station (or Friargate straight

ahead, taking in the restored friary remains, now a pleasant Youth Hostel, from which you can cut through the attractive new housing estate to the station instead).

PUB INFORMATION

1 **DOG & DUCK**
33 Ladygate, Beverley, HU17 8BH •
01482 862419 • www.bedandbreakfastbeverley.com
Opening hours: 11-4, 7-midnight; 11-midnight Fri & Sat; 11.30-3, 7-11 Sun

2 **WHITE HORSE (NELLIE'S)**
22 Hengate, Beverley, HU17 8BL
01482 861973 • www.nellies.co.uk
Opening hours: 11-11; 12-10.30 Sun

3 **CHEQUERS MICROPUB**
15 Swaby's Yard, Dyer Lane, Beverley, HU17 9BZ
07964 227906 • www.chequersmicropub.co.uk
Opening hours: closed Mon; 12-11 (10 Tue & Wed); 12-10 Sun

4 **WOOLPACK**
37 Westwood Road, Beverley, HU17 8EN
01482 867095
Opening hours: 4.30-10.30 Mon; 12-3, 4.30-11; 12-11 Sat & Sun

5 **TIGER INN**
Lairgate, Beverley, HU17 8JG
01482 869040 • www.tiger-inn-beverley.co.uk
Opening hours: closed Mon; 11-11 (midnight Fri & Sat); 12-11 Sun

Try also:

6 **CORNERHOUSE**
2 Norwood, Beverley, HU17 9ET
01482 882652
Opening hours: closed Mon; 5-midnight (1am Fri); 10-1am Sat; 10-11 Sun

Hull's old town: a fishy trail

With the possible exception of York, the old port city of Hull is perhaps the most enjoyable of Yorkshire's larger towns and cities for a pub walk, and with one big advantage: you can have the place almost to yourself at many times of the week. The historic centre of the once pre-eminent fishing port has been left largely in peace as the modern Central Business district has migrated west, and it's here that most of the interest, and the best pubs, are to be found. Pub architecture aficionados should pack their copy of *Yorkshire's Real Heritage Pubs* before departing for Hull as several of the pubs have architectural interest. There's plenty to see throughout the trail as well, so it's not so surprising that Hull is preparing for its year in the sun as UK City of Culture in 2017. An added attraction of the walk is that it follows quite closely the Hull Fish Trail, and I strongly recommend you pick up a leaflet about this from the tourist office in Queen Victoria Square before you start.

▶ **Start/finish:** Hull railway station

▶ **Distance:** 3.2 miles (5.3 km) from and to station

▶ **Key attractions:** Historic old city; transport and other museums; The Deep (aquarium)

▶ **THE PUBS:** Olde White Harte, Minerva Hotel, Lion & Key, Wm Hawkes, Olde Black Boy, Hop & Vine. Try also: Kingston, White Hart (currently closed)

▶ **Timing tips:** On Monday and Tuesday the Olde Black Boy is closed until 5.30pm; the Hop & Vine is also closed on Sunday and Monday. Try one of the other days!

Humber Dock Marina

KEY

🚶 Walk start/finish

⊪⊪⊪ Walk route

WEST STREET

JAMESON STR

Hull Station

PARAGON STRE

FERENSWAY

ANLABY ROAD

The Kingston and Trinity House in the heart of the old town

🚶 Readers arriving in Hull by train or bus should make their way down to Queen Victoria Square – probably the strongest candidate for the centre of town – with its imposing statue of Her Majesty and enclosed by notable architecture including the City Hall and the old dock company offices, now the maritime museum. Here you will also find the Tourist Information Centre (for information on the Fish Trail). To the south of the square is Princes Quay shopping centre, partially built over the old Princes Dock, which had lain derelict for many years. As you walk down alongside the water on Princes Dock Street, you'll see that leisure is now the order of the day, even more so in the marina ahead. Pass handsome Roland House on your left: this was built in 1822 as the Robinson Almshouses.

At the old sugar mill warehouse (now a nightclub), turn left into Posterngate, which still carries a strong flavour of old Hull. Pass the old Seamen's Mission (now a pub and nightclub) and reach the junction at Trinity Square. The handsome exterior of the

7 Kingston is ahead of you, and you may wish to include this pub on your itinerary, especially at a quieter time. Expect three beers from the Marston's stable, and note the impressive bar back (sadly most of the other old fittings have been stripped out).

The square is dominated by the huge bulk of the Church of the Holy Trinity, the largest and arguably the most magnificent Parish Church in England. The present building is the third church built on this site and was founded in 1285, with the last building work consecrated in 1425. Unusually for a church of this age and importance, it is substantially built of brick. Note also Trinity House opposite the pub, part of an extensive religious guild founded in 1369, but later becoming associated with and symbolising Hull's maritime greatness; it was described by Daniel Defoe in his *Tour Through the Whole Island of Great Britain* as 'the Glory of the Town'. The present building dates to 1753.

Courtyard at the Olde White Harte

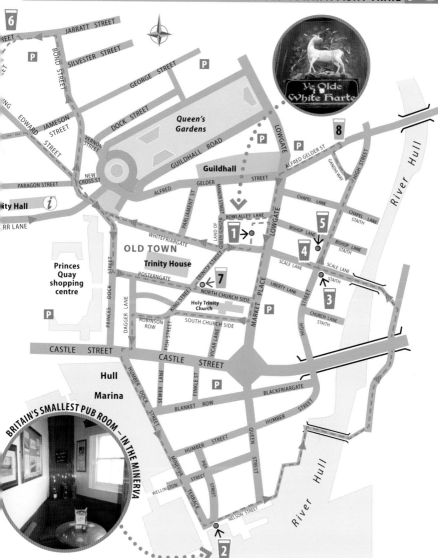

Turn right at the next corner (by the William Wilberforce, a Wetherspoon pub) into Silver Street and look for the sign of the **1 Olde White Harte** on your left. One of Hull's oldest pubs, it lies down an alley off the street, accessed from an atmospheric little courtyard. Refurbished in an 'Old English' style in the late 19th century, the interior retains some elements of its former domestic life, including large fireplaces, and the upstairs function rooms, notably the 'Plotting Room', a dubious Civil War reference. Only one bar is in regular use, dispensing a range of Theakston beers, plus Caley Deuchars IPA and one or two guests. Note the very pretty decorative glasswork, as well as the attractive wood bar fronts; and the little built-in phone booth to the left-hand 'smoke room'.

Continue through the passageway, turning right into Bowlalley Lane and right again on

Minerva

Lion & Key

the main road, Lowgate. There are two things of note on the right as you stroll down here. The attractive Hepworth's Arcade is a listed Victorian covered shopping mall, which once housed a very early penny bazaar of Mssrs Marks & Spencer. There's an entrance to the indoor market from the arcade, but this can also be reached a few doors further down Lowgate from the alley that leads to the Olde Blue Ball – pub heritage enthusiasts might wish to drop in here for its multi-roomed layout and a nice little snug with its original fitted seating. Whether or not you visit this and/or the market, return to Lowgate and continue beyond the Trinity Church to South Church Side, where you need to turn right and walk alongside the church to the south side of Trinity Square once again. Note the old red brick grammar school, a 16th-century Tudor building whose most noted alumnus is probably William Wilberforce.

Bear left by the old Merchants Warehouse and right into cobbled Robinson Row. Bear left at the end and walk down to busy Castle Street, which you should negotiate by the crossing. Humber Dock promenade leads you alongside the former outer dock, now converted to a marina but retaining some attractive old maritime buildings around it. Set in a display case on the pavement is a horizontal steam engine used to draw up

vessels from the Humber for repair and fitting out. In clear weather you can see across the Humber to the oil refinery in Lincolnshire, but much closer, just past the (greatly expanded) Green Bricks pub, and before reaching the end of the street and the Minerva, look out for the impressive swordfish set into the pavement. Located close to the old pier and ferry terminus, the old **2** **Minerva Hotel** is a very welcome refuge at all times but never more so than in adverse weather. Sadly the pier is quiet now and no ferries run, but you can look at a fascinating array of old photographs inside the pub. The place, which retains some of its old Tetley badging, still has plenty of character and boasts what is billed as Britain's smallest pub room. Alongside so-called Tetley Cask, from Northampton these days (!), there are several other beers on the counter; and an extensive food service is available if you want to lunch here, which is probably a good option.

Continue anticlockwise along the quay towards the futuristic aquarium known as 'The Deep', and along the River Hull walkway passing the former dry dock site (under redevelopment at the time of writing) and cross the new footbridge to The Deep. Swing left (inland) under the flyover and head up to the even newer (2013) Scale Lane pedestrian swing bridge, which carries you right back into the heart of historic old Hull. You now have a plethora of good drinking options almost literally within a stone's throw. Take in as many as you like. On the immediate corner is the **3 Lion & Key**, with its original name now tastefully restored, and 'repositioned' as a comfortable alehouse serving an extensive food menu – though it's the fish and chips that get the rave reviews. The eclectic interior is characterful and offers a range of 'seating experiences', whilst in good weather the enclosed courtyard is a pleasant space as well. You won't be short of choice on the ale front with more than a dozen handpumps on the bar; real cider is also available.

A few doors further up Scale Lane straight ahead of you, and opposite the Manchester Arms, is **4 Wm Hawkes**. Converted to pub use from a former gun maker's and printer's shop in 2012, if there's a more authentic-looking creation of an intimate, old-fashioned atmosphere than in this little gem, I have yet to see it. Dark wood (much of it reclaimed, like the windows) abounds, and the front room is full of all sorts of clutter on every surface. Expect a fine selection of changing ales (and a real cider) on nine handpumps.

Just a little further up the road is Walters, offering another fine range of well-kept

beers with a focus on microbreweries, served in a smart café-bar interior, but for a more atmospheric and frankly unmissable stop-off, return to the Lion & Key and bear left into the High Street, where you'll come across the **5 Olde Black Boy** almost immediately. Hull High Street these days is a quiet backwater, and the Olde Black Boy is a rare survivor of the once numerous licensed premises on what was once the main thoroughfare in town. The current interior is almost a century old but has the feel of greater antiquity; indeed, the place was a wine merchants in Victorian times, and the front 'smoke room' was converted from the office. This little room hosts impromptu folk sessions at times, but the rear room is more spacious. Half a dozen changing real ales (and Weston's Olde Rosie Cider) are available, along with bar snacks. If you're pushed for time, it's possible to continue the trail more directly by making for the Hop & Vine via Bishop Lane (see map), but I would recommend the route described here. Continue up the High Street into what Hull's masters now like to call the 'museum quarter'. At least there are museums in it, and perhaps the best is the Streetlife Museum of Transport (free admission) on the right, just five minutes from the Olde Black Boy.

Wm Hawkes

The Maritime Museum on Queen Victoria Square

Hop & Vine

Just beyond Streetlife is Wilberforce House, now a museum of the slave trade, just as you bear left into Gandhi Way to join Alfred Gelder Street. Across the road here is the **8 White Hart** (if it has been re-opened), which deserves its 'try also' rating, whatever the beer, for its very classy frontage and superb front lounge with its rare ceramic-fronted bar counter. Unfortunately its future at the time of writing is distinctly uncertain, and all you may be able to see is the exterior.

From here, turn back towards the city centre. Although it's quicker to keep straight ahead to return to Queen Victoria Square, it's more interesting to turn left down Lowgate

and, passing the Three John Scotts (a good Wetherspoon house), turn right again into Bowlalley Lane, left into the curiously named Land of Green Ginger – nobody quite knows where the name comes from – and then right down pedestrianised Whitefriargate. From the square it's but five more minutes to the last official stop of the day. Head northwards up Savile Street and straight across into Bond Street, cutting across the car park if you wish, which will bring you out on Albion Street pretty much opposite the basement bar at the **6 Hop & Vine**. Look for the sign above the railings on the wall. This little award-winning bar is a great addition to Hull's real ale scene and makes a good finale to a rewarding trip. The three cask beers change regularly and the website will tell you what's on and upcoming; cider drinkers are very well catered for, too, as evidenced by a finalists' position in CAMRA's 2014 Cider Pub of the Year competition. In addition, there are some bottled Belgian offerings and draft Czech beers including Budvar Dark. And chances are you may be feeling peckish again by now, so ask about the home-prepared food, available until 9pm. It's only five minutes back to the station: consult your map and/or ask at the bar for directions.

PUB INFORMATION

1 OLDE WHITE HARTE
25 Silver Street, Hull, HU1 1JG
01482 326363 • www.yeoldewhiteharte.com
Opening hours: 11-midnight (1am Fri & Sat);
12-midnight Sun

2 MINERVA HOTEL
Nelson Street, Hull, HU1 1XE
01482 210025 • www.minerva-hull.co.uk
Opening hours: 11.30-11.30

3 LION & KEY
48 High Street, Hull, HU1 1QE
01482 225212
Opening hours: 11.30-11

4 WM HAWKES
32 Scale Lane, Hull, HU1 1LF
01482 224004 • www.wmhawkes.co.uk
Opening hours: 12-11

5 OLDE BLACK BOY
150 High Street, Hull, HU1 1PS
01482 326516 • yeoldeblackboy.weebly.com
Opening hours: 12.30 (5 Mon-Wed)-11.30

6 HOP & VINE
24 Albion Street, Hull, HU1 3TH
07500 543199 • www.hopandvinehull.co.uk
Opening hours: closed Mon; 11 (4 Tue)-11; 11-11.30
Fri & Sat; closed Sun

Try also:

7 KINGSTON
25 Trinity House Lane, Hull HU1 2JA
01482 223635
Opening hours: 11-11

8 WHITE HART
109 Alfred Gelder Street, Hull, HU1 1EP
(currently closed)

PUB INDEX

Buck Inn, Buckden p33

White Horse (Nellie's), Beverley p161

Blind Jack's, Knaresborough p55

Black Horse, Whitby p73

Old Silent, Stanbury p86

Brigantes, York p145

BEER INDEX

Sair Inn, Linthwaite p93

BOOKS FOR BEER LOVERS

CAMRA Books, the publishing arm of the Campaign for Real Ale, is the leading publisher of books on beer and pubs. Key titles include:

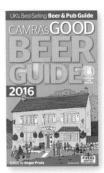

GOOD BEER GUIDE 2016

Editor: Roger Protz

CAMRA's *Good Beer Guide* is fully revised and updated each year and features pubs across the United Kingdom that serve the best real ale. Now in its 43rd edition, this pub guide is completely independent with listings based entirely on nomination and evaluation by CAMRA members. This means you can be sure that every one of the 4,500 pubs deserves their place, plus they all come recommended by people who know a thing or two about good beer.

£15.99   ISBN 978-1-85249-327-1

SO YOU WANT TO BE A BEER EXPERT?

Jeff Evans

More people than ever are searching for an understanding of what makes a great beer, and this book meets that demand by presenting a hands-on course in beer appreciation, with sections on understanding the beer styles of the world, beer flavours, how beer is made, the ingredients, and more. Uniquely, *So You Want to Be a Beer Expert?* doesn't just relate the facts, but helps readers reach conclusions for themselves. Key to this are the interactive tastings that show readers, through their own taste-buds, what beer is all about. CAMRA's *So You Want to Be a Beer Expert?* is the ideal book, for anyone who wants to further their knowledge and enjoyment of beer.

£12.99   ISBN 978-1-85249-322-6

BRITAIN'S BEST REAL HERITAGE PUBS

Geoff Brandwood

This full-colour guide lists 270 pubs throughout the UK that have interiors of real historic significance – some over a century old. Illustrated with high-quality photography, the book's extensive listings are the product of years of surveying and research by CAMRA's Pub Heritage Group, which is dedicated to preserving and protecting our rich pub heritage. The book features a forward by Simon Thurley, Chief Executive of English Heritage.

£9.99   ISBN 978-1-85249-304-2

YORKSHIRE'S REAL HERITAGE PUBS

Dave Gamston

This unique guide will lead you to the pubs in Yorkshire and Humber which still have interiors or internal features of real historic significance. Over 100 entries range from simple rural 'time warp' pubs to ornate Victorian drinking 'palaces', and include some of the more unsung pub interiors from the inter-war and later years that we take so much for granted. *Yorkshire's Real Heritage Pubs* is the first guide of its kind for Yorkshire. Originally published in 2011 and now fully updated and re-launched in the revised edition, it champions the need to celebrate, understand and protect the genuine pub heritage that remains to us.

£4.99   **ISBN 978-1-85249-315-8**

LONDON PUB WALKS

Bob Steel

CAMRA's pocket-size walking guide to London is back. This fantastic second edition is packed with interesting new routes, fully updated classic routes from the first edition, new pubs and a special selection of routes that take full advantage of London's public transport network. With 30 walks around more than 190 pubs, CAMRA's *London Pub Walks* enables you to explore the entire city while never being far from a decent pint.

£9.99   **ISBN 978-1-85249-310-3**

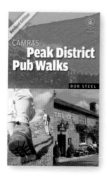

PEAK DISTRICT PUB WALKS

Bob Steel

A practical pocket-sized traveller's guide to some of the best pubs and best walking in the Peak District. This book features 25 walks, as well as cycle routes and local attractions, helping you see the best of Britain's oldest National Park while never straying too far from a decent pint. Each route has been selected for its inspiring landscape, historical interest and welcoming pubs.

£9.99   **ISBN 978-1-85249-246-5**

Order these and other CAMRA books online at **www.camra.org. uk/books**, ask at your local bookstore, or contact: CAMRA, 230 Hatfield Road, St Albans, AL1 4LW.

Telephone 01727 867201

A CAMPAIGN OF TWO HALVES

Campaigning for Pub Goers & Beer Drinkers

CAMRA, the Campaign for Real Ale, is the not-for-profit independent voice of real ale drinkers and pub goers. CAMRA's vision is to have quality real ale and thriving pubs in every community. We campaign tirelessly to achieve this goal, as well as lobbying government to champion drinkers' rights. As a CAMRA member you will have the opportunity to campaign to save pubs under threat of closure, for pubs to be free to serve a range of real ales at fair prices and for a long-term freeze in beer duty that will help Britain's brewing industry survive.

Enjoying Real Ale & Pubs

CAMRA has over 175,000 members from all ages and backgrounds, brought together by a common belief in the issues that CAMRA deals with and their love of good quality British beer. From just £24 a year* – that's less than a pint a month – you can join CAMRA and enjoy the following benefits:

- Subscription to *What's Brewing*, our monthly colour newspaper, and *Beer*, our quarterly magazine, informing you about beer and pub news and detailing events and beer festivals around the country.

- Free or reduced entry to over 160 national, regional and local beer festivals.

- Money off many of our publications including the *Good Beer Guide*, the *Good Bottled Beer Guide* and *So You Want to Be a Beer Expert?*

- Access to a members-only section of our website, **www.camra.org.uk**, which gives up-to-the-minute news stories and includes a special offer section with regular features.

- Special discounts with numerous partner organisations and money off real ale in your participating local pubs as part of our Pubs Discount Scheme.

Log onto **www.camra.org.uk/join** for CAMRA membership information.

*£24 membership cost stated is only available via Direct Debit, other concessionary rates available. Please note membership rates stated are correct at the time of printing but are subject to change. Full details of all membership rates can be found here: **www.camra.org.uk/membershiprates**